Gielgoodies!

Gielgoodies!

& Gaffes
The Wit and Wisdom/of John Gielgud

Compiled by
Jonathan Croall

Prologue by
Simon Callow

OBERON BOOKS

LONDON

Contents

Sources and Acknowledgements

The majority of the items included here come from the two hundred interviews I conducted for my two biographies *Gielgud: A Theatrical Life* (2000) and *John Gielgud: Matinee Idol to Movie Star* (2011). For both books I had regretfully to exclude a good many jewels, so I welcome the opportunity to record them for posterity. I am grateful once again to all those many people who relished passing on to me so many gems.

Several items have been taken from Gielgud's letters, many unpublished, and from interviews he gave to journalists. I have indicated the source at the end of each item, using the following code: L = Letter, I = Interview, M = Memoir, B = Biography, D = Diary, U = Unknown, S = Several sources. All other items were given to me personally, either during my interviews or, in a few cases, by letter or e-mail.

I am grateful to everyone who responded to my requests for contributions, which were published in the *Stage*, the *Equity Journal* and the *Daily Telegraph*. I must also thank the trustees of John Gielgud's estate for permission to quote from his letters and other copyright material, and the following for the cartoons: Surra (page 17), Nerman (27), Ronald Searle (33 and 87), Nona (55), Vicky (63), Clive Francis (95), Trog (103), Gary (125) and Ferguson (133).

Clive Francis

Introduction

'I think an actor who is too solemn about his work is really rather a bore.'

John Gielgud was not just a great actor: he was also a formidable wit, a brilliant raconteur – and a very naughty boy.

He was, in more senses than one, a man of many parts. In researching my two biographies of Gielgud, I gradually discovered a fascinating mixture of elements in his absorbingly complex personality. There was first and foremost the sensitive, intelligent and dedicated man of the theatre, determined to perfect his art and serve his public. There was also the mercurial director with the butterfly mind, prone to test his actors' patience to the limit with his continual, often bizarre changes of mind.

But I also encountered a deliciously flippant and wicked side to his nature. It was to be found in his perennial love of scandal and gossip, his schoolboy delight in sexual and scatological jokes, his lightning wit and bawdy humour, his scurrilous portraits of his friends and colleagues, and his delight in language in general and puns in particular. Such qualities are to be greatly treasured. But he was also cherished for those gaffes, bricks and clangers affectionately known as 'Gielgoofs' or, more commonly, 'Gielgoodies', which are here celebrated in all their glory.

The bricks that he dropped were legion, and a direct consequence of his quicksilver mind and wildly impulsive nature. Somehow he lacked that useful skill of self-censorship that most of us have, that crucial ability to think before we speak: no sooner had a thought entered his brain than it came tumbling out of his mouth. It was a lifelong habit that prompted Tennessee Williams to label him 'that famous London Brick Factory', while Kenneth Tynan suggested he had 'dropped bricks enough to re-build the Globe theatre'. Gielgud had his own image, confessing to Emlyn Williams: 'I seem to have dropped enough bricks to build a new Wall of China. Well, so long as I don't offend, I don't mind making a fool of myself.'

Amazingly, he didn't generally offend. His friends, family and colleagues so loved or admired him, they not only tolerated his appalling tactlessness, but actually relished it. Paul Scofield told me: 'If you don't know him his *mots* can sound cruel and empty, whereas in his mouth they are innocent and inconsequential and very funny. Most of those who worked with him at one time or another were his victims, though not, I think, his targets, and there can be few who had not forgiven, if not forgotten, by the end of the day.' His view is supported by Judi Dench, who suggested to me that 'his bricks came out of an incredible shyness and were unintentional'. Alec Guinness, who remembered him being 'hopelessly tactless and unintentionally cruel', said he believed the gaffes were 'entirely forgivable, because they sprang spontaneously from the heart without a glimmer of malice'.

His most celebrated gaffe concerned the wonderfully named playwright Eddie Knoblock. It was a moment Gielgud himself recalled when he was a guest on *Desert Island Discs*. 'He was very kind to me as a young man, and I used to know him very well,' he explained. 'He wrote a successful play called *Kismet*, but towards the end of his life he was very unsuccessful, and I think he lost all his money. We were lunching at the Ivy one day. He said he had twenty-five unpublished plays in his top drawer, and he talked on and on. I said about someone else: "He's almost a big a bore as Eddie Knoblock." To his face! I didn't know *what* to do. I can hear myself saying it now. I do hope he wasn't too upset.'

Far from being upset, many of his victims, including the luckless Jill Bennett and Clive Morton, and several of those actors and directors whom I interviewed for my biography, positively enjoyed dining out on the stories featuring themselves as the victim of his careless tongue. But not everyone was convinced that all the bricks were dropped by accident. One member of this small dissident minority was Robert Stephens, who said: 'I'm sure that once he knew he could get away with something like that, it's possible that some of them were a little tongue-in-cheek.' Could there be some truth in his opinion? The feast of Gielgoodies prepared here provides plenty of food for thought.

As with many theatrical stories, those featuring Gielgud have often been altered or embroidered over the years, as in a game of Chinese Whispers. The best-known concern Clive Morton, who seems to have been 'Knoblocked' in at least three different places, in Gielgud's dressing-room, the

BBC canteen, and the street, and the veteran actress Athene Seyler, whose wounding either took place in a recording studio or at a dinner party – but surely not in both places?

The theatre is notorious for its apocryphal stories, and I have excluded any which seemed obviously so. I have also refused entry to those where I suspected the teller had naughtily inserted themselves into a tale which I knew belonged to someone else. In passing I have aimed to clear up several historical inaccuracies, such as the common assertion that Gielgud's famous put-down of Richard Burton's performance of Hamlet took place in America in 1964 (it was actually at the Old Vic in 1953). Where there have been competing versions of the same story, I have given preference to the more reliable first-hand testimony.

Compiling this celebratory volume has been a hugely enjoyable task. I hope it does justice to Gielgud's vividly engaging personality, to a giant of the theatre who was certainly one of the wittiest men of his time, if not always the wisest.

Prologue
by Simon Callow

John was like a fountain, a splendid, rococo fountain in the grounds of a Schönbrunn or a Versailles: burbling, sparkling, never gushing, but quite unstoppable. And in those delicious effusions all sorts of unexpected and eye-raising droplets would scatter themselves about. Shocking scurrility, devastating criticism, scandalous indiscretion would pour joyously out in a headlong spurt, alongside tender reminiscences and moments of great nobility. It was a little discombobulating, a sort of Lewis Carroll world of absurd association and non sequitur, a mind quite uncensored, in instant contact with itself, surprised by sudden accesses of mirth or of emotion, the surrealism of the stream of consciousness that poured from his mouth only heightened by the speaker's impeccable sartorial formality and bearing, and the exquisitely inflected bassoonish tones in which it was all delivered.

My first encounter with him was, fittingly, in a dressing room. It was the Duke of York's theatre, the play was *Half-Life* by Julian Mitchell, and the room was crowded with friends and well-wishers. I was a young actor, brought by an older friend who knew John. I hung back politely, but John made no distinctions between people: the contents of his mind came pouring out indiscriminately at whoever might be standing in front of him.

'I've left the house in Cowley Street and moved to the country, you know,' he told me. 'Nobody gives parties in London any more, don't you find?' 'Um,' I said. But he was already off. 'I managed to see Ingrid in her show the other night before we transferred – do you think our play will go? It's a bit *recherché*, don't you think? I don't understand half of what I have to say in it – and I was very disappointed by the whole thing, dreadful sets, so ugly, like a great big penny farthing, quite hopeless, and her performance was terribly misjudged. Poor, dear Ingrid – fluent in five languages and she can't act in any of them.' He gurgled with delight at this *aperçu* and then he was off again. 'Oh, I did laugh when they found the Bishop of Winchester with his trousers round his ankles and the postman on his knees', a reference bewildering to everyone – Was it from a play? A novel? The Sunday papers? – but by now he was remembering Rubinstein playing Chopin in the late 1920s, and his eyes suddenly welled up with tears.

Nothing that had happened on stage that evening was remotely as entertaining, as stimulating, or as touching as what poured out of him during those thirty minutes in the dressing room. It was like running across the White Rabbit – but a White Rabbit that had read all of Proust and acted half of Shakespeare, and was drenched in poetry and music and art. The raffishness and the naughtiness and the delight in gossip, ancient and modern, belonged to another century; and yet, however sharp the barbs seemed, the presiding atmosphere was of sheer *joie de vivre*, of irrepressible exuberance. There was boyishness and silliness, to be sure; but there was no malice. The Mozartian music of his voice cast a sparkle and an elegance over everything.

I had known him at a distance when I was in the box office at the Old Vic while he was briefly a member of the company during the National Theatre's tenure under Olivier, and his sayings were gleefully reported. On seeing the set for Peter Brook's troubled but ultimately triumphant production of Seneca's *Oedipus*, for instance, with its golden walls and its giant phallus, he had said, without a moment's hesitation: 'Cox and Box'. It was much later that I got to know him personally, first through the generous letters he would write to me about my books as each appeared. These (invariably hand-written) epistles were instantly recognisable from their tapering paragraphs, disappearing off the edge of the page, and they were every bit as indiscreetly effervescent as his conversation. A comment in one of them about the Irish actor Micheál MacLíammóir led seamlessly to a delicious reminiscence about being groped by MacLíammóir's partner Hilton Edwards at the Old Vic in 1927 under the fortunately unseeing gaze of Lilian Baylis; his gossip from the past was as fresh as if it had just happened yesterday.

In addition I had occasion to interview him, from time to time, about various people – Charles Laughton, for example ('Poor Laughton! I believe that at the end he had to have lorry drivers shipped over to him from the East Coast'), and indeed MacLíammóir, famous for his street make-up and toupee: 'I could never understand why he wasn't arrested,' exclaimed John. His candour was not just reserved for people: it applied equally to plays. 'What a dreadful bore *Heartbreak House* is!' he once said to me, of the play often considered to be Shaw's masterpiece, and in which he had played Captain Shotover on television. 'I went to the first performance at the Royal Court in 1921, and if it hadn't been for the bomb in the last act, we'd all still be there now, fast asleep.'

Productions were equally liable to be shot down. He said to me during the course of the interview about Laughton that there were no parts that he, John, longed to play anymore, except for Sir George Sitwell. But that wouldn't happen now because some dreadful play about Edith and Sacheverell and Osbert and the family had opened the night before at the Lyric theatre in Hammersmith. 'I directed it, John,' I said. 'Did you?' he replied. 'Is it as bad as they all say?' (The play had, in fact, had rather good notices.) On another occasion I was with the producer Michael Codron at the Garrick Club. Codron's parents had both just died in a freak accident. John caught sight of him and came rushing over. 'Oh, Michael,' he said, 'something dreadful's just happened to you, what is it?' Quite impossible to take offence.

The book you have in your hand is a glorious compendium of John's scintillating irreverences and fabulous *faux pas*. They were as much a part of him as his more sublime and lofty utterances, and they wonderfully convey a sense of what it was like to be around him. He was one of the greatest of all theatrical personalities, and these utterly characteristic throwaway squibs bring him vividly back to life.

Gielgoodies:
Actors and Playwrights

Some of his excruciating gaffes were at the expense of star actors. But many others in his companies also suffered.

Timothy Bateson
Richard Burton was playing Hamlet at the Old Vic, but he was very nervous and not at his best. John came round to his dressing-room afterwards, to find him stark naked. 'I'm so sorry, Richard,' he said. 'Shall I come back when you're better – I mean when you're dressed?'

To Vivien Leigh, after she suggested playing a scene
from Romeo and Juliet for a wartime concert party:
Oh no, Vivien! Only a great actress
can do that sort of thing. (B)

*To Alec Guinness, then a rising young star,
on meeting him in Piccadilly:*
I can't think why you want to play big parts. Why don't you stick to the little people you do so well? *(M)*

Ronald Pickup
I had taken over from Tom Courtenay in *The Norman Conquests*, not very successfully. 'Sorry I didn't see your play,' he said. 'I heard the new cast was a disaster.'

To Emlyn Williams, after seeing his one-man show on Dylan Thomas:
Your breath control is so much better. None of that gasping and gulping when you played Richard III at the Old Vic. (M)

John Mills
We were rehearsing *Charley's Aunt* at the Haymarket. I was running around the stage in this heavy black frock, with my wig all over the place. At the end of the first act I went down to the footlights and said: 'How was it, Johnnie?' And he said: 'Interminable, my dear fellow, absolutely interminable.'

Robert Lang
Olivier once invited me to dinner with Gielgud. During the meal he asked Gielgud: 'Did you ever read Ionesco's *Rhinoceros*, which I played at the Royal Court?' Gielgud said: 'Yes I did, it was offered to me first.' I got the impression this was news to Olivier.

Pinkie Johnstone
After the read-through of *The School for Scandal*, he said to me: 'Pinkie, you're meant to be like a little ping-pong ball dancing on top of a fountain, but you're like a slow drip of cold water.'

Robin Phillips
I was driving him to a rehearsal of *Caesar and Cleopatra* at Chichester, and he was talking about the cast. 'Pat Nye is a dear, but frankly Harold Innocent doesn't stand a chance. That old crocodile will eat him for the coffee break long before we get to opening night. She was in the war, you know, as a Wren. I wouldn't have liked to face that Dreadnought across the Channel, would you?'

Michael Denison
After I acted in his OUDS production of *Richard II* at Oxford,
I wrote to him to ask him what he thought my chances might
be of joining the profession. He replied saying: 'There are
already many more actors than there are positions available
in any one season, and perhaps your abilities would point to
success in some other profession.'

Peter Copley
When I was seventeen I was taken to see him in *Richard of
Bordeaux*, and afterwards introduced to him. In my
well-mannered public-school way I said: 'It's a tremendous
honour to meet you.' And he said: 'Don't be such a
bloody fool!'

Dulcie Gray
We were sharing a taxi once. I said: 'I believe you were
at school with all my uncles.' 'No I wasn't!' he said,
without inquiring who they were.

*To Trader Faulkner, during rehearsals
for* The Lady's Not for Burning:
You're so pretty, but that dreadful voice! There's a terrible
compost in your vowels.

To Walter ('Dickie') Hudd, reminiscing over lunch:
Dear Bobby Harris, a frightfully nice fellow, but terribly bitter, he feels he never made it. You're not bitter are you, Dickie? *(Richard Bebb)*

Michael Craig

Cedric Messina was casting Shaw's *In Good King Charles' Golden Days* for television. Gielgud said to him: 'James is such a boring part. Why don't you offer it to Michael Craig?'

To Gordon Honeycombe,
who suggested while
they were rehearsing the
newsreader's adaptation of
Paradise Lost *that he should*
deliver a line with a rising inflection:
I suppose I might say it like that
if it were the nine o'clock news.
(Martin Jarvis)

To Emlyn Williams, while casting a radio play:
Stephen Haggard is splendid, but *much* too well-bred. It calls for an actor who would convey somebody savage, uncouth – Emlyn, *you* should be playing it! *(M)*

ຕ

Several leading playwrights found the quality of their work being called into question.

Charles Wood
We were casting my play *Veterans* in Michael Codron's office. Someone suggested Geraldine McEwan. John said: 'Oh no, she's far too grand now. She doesn't do anything unless it's absolutely first class.'

In the hearing of Julian Mitchell, during rehearsals for his play Half-Life*:*
We can cut some of this rubbish; it's too long. *(Frances Cuka)*

To Alan Bennett, who made many changes to Forty Years On *during its provincial tour:*
David Storey was the ideal author: he just sat there and didn't say a word.

To the actors rehearsing Spring, 1600, *while sitting next to its creator Emlyn Williams:*
Sorry everybody, but you're all being too slow. We must get it tearing along at this point. Emlyn agrees with me that from now on his last act is thin. *(M)*

*To Terence Rattigan, discussing whether he should
appear in a double bill of his new plays:*
They've seen me in so much first-rate stuff, do you really
think they will like me in anything second-rate? *(B)*

Peter Shaffer
During the run of my play *The Shrivings* Wendy Hiller
said she wanted her part cut, because she was liable to
miss her last train to Beaconsfield. John said: 'You can
cut my part if you want, I wouldn't mind at all.'

☙

Even a loyal fan could become one of his victims.

Richard Johnson
On tour he was followed around by a faithful posse of ladies
of a certain age, who so regularly collected his autograph on
every provincial theatre programme that he came to know
many of them by sight, and sometimes even by name. One day,
emerging from the stage door after a matinee, he found a lady
who had a pronounced astigmatism studying the posters and
photos displayed along the wall. 'Hullo, Mrs Brown!' he greeted
her. 'Having a squint at the posters, are you?'

1

The Butterfly Mind

At a dress rehearsal of *Macbeth*:
'I'm so sorry everybody.
I'm just the most terrible director.'

*As a director he was imaginative, restless
and mercurial, leaving many actors in despair because
of his notorious tendency to change his mind from one
moment to the next. As he once remarked to the theatre
critic Robert Muller: 'The moment one makes a decision,
life becomes quite unbearably dull.'*

Peter Shaffer

During the first rehearsal of my play *Five-Finger Exercise*, he gave the actors a different move for every single line of the first two scenes, so they were running around the stage like a team of performing mice on amphetamine. After lunch he said: 'Let's run it, it will be amusing.' So they did, and he said: 'What are you all doing? It's a nightmare!' And Brian Bedford said: 'We're trying to do the moves you've given us.' And John said: 'What on earth for? Everyone knows I can't direct.'

Watching the final scene of Macbeth *during a dress rehearsal:*
We'll have to change the whole thing: it's too much like
White Horse Inn. (John Nettleton)

To the company, after a preview of his Broadway production of Hamlet*:*
I've made a terrible mistake. It all lacks colour and majesty, and it's my fault. Tomorrow night you'll all wear capes! *(Richard L Sterne)*

Wendy Hiller

During the dress-rehearsal for *The Cradle Song* he was pacing up and down in thought. We started to chatter a bit, and he suddenly called out: 'Be quiet everyone, I'm in a frenzy!'

☙

He was never a great believer in investigating the psychology of a character.

John McCallum
When Richard Wordsworth asked him to explain the Duke of York's lines in *Richard II,* 'As in a theatre, the eyes of men, / After a well-graced actor leaves the stage, / Are idly bent on him that enters next,' John replied: 'It's very simple, dear boy. It's when Paul Scofield goes off and you come on.'

To Sarah Miles, during rehearsals for Dazzling Prospect*:*
I'm so sorry everybody. I'm just the most terrible director.

Jonathan Cecil
During the run of *Halfway Up the Tree* I overheard Robert Morley telling him that he didn't understand a certain scene. 'Neither do I,' he replied, 'but I think it's awfully good – terribly Chekhovian.'

John McCallum
While he was rehearsing *Much Ado About Nothing* in America, one young actor asked him: 'Who am I, where do I come from?' And John said: 'You come from the wings. Now get on with it.'

❦

His suggestions and notes to actors varied from the forthright to the bizarre.

To Michael Bryant, during rehearsals of Five-Finger Exercise*:*
You've got to cut that speech in front of the mirror, otherwise the audience will think you've gone over there to wash your balls.

Hume Cronyn
While rehearsing *Hamlet* in America he was struggling to stage a scene involving Claudius and his courtiers. Things weren't going well. The stage picture would not come right. John's voice rose above the rest: 'No, no, no! It's terrible, quite terrible....Coolidge, wear a hat!' *(M)*

Geoffrey Bayldon
During one rehearsal for *The Way of the World* he said to me: 'Go to the left side of him. No, come in again. Go to the right side of him. He's a comic character, think of something that's funny.' By now the company was massing in the wings. Then he said: 'Go round him. No, not round his *body*. Round *him*. Oh, let's stop there.' I never knew what he meant.

Michael Allinson
He was directing Ingrid Bergman in Somerset Maugham's *The Constant Wife*. According to the author's stage direction, my character Bernard was supposed to kiss her passionately. But John said to me: 'Oh Michael, do it *tactfully*!'

To Mavis Walker, during rehearsals for The Chalk Garden*:*
Wouldn't it be fun if the maid had a laugh like the sound of a teaspoon tinkling in a medicine glass.

To Denis Quilley, rehearsing a scene in The Lady's Not for Burning*:*
It's very Norman and rounded, Squilley. Can we get it a little more Gothic and pointed?

Peter Ustinov
During rehearsals for my play *Halfway Up the Tree* I said to him: 'There's no conflict in that scene, the girl must be more brutal with her mother.' He listened with great interest, and then said: 'Yes, perhaps I should have allowed her to wear a hat after all.'

ॐ

He liked to tell friends of his difficulties
handling actors in rehearsals.

To Hugh Wheeler, on Ralph Richardson and his wife Meriel Forbes,
whom he was rehearsing in The School for Scandal:
I struggle with the somewhat recalcitrant chums at the
Haymarket – the Richardsons really are a rather tough nut
to crack, the one the best Brazil, the other an anthracite
brick (Madame, needless to say). *(L)*

To Paul Anstee, while rehearsing his production of Big Fish, Little Fish:
The cast is quite excellent, though Jason Robards is rather
behind-hand owing to nightly potations, which makes him
slow to learn. He is awfully good and very sweet in many
ways, but a big spoilt baby, like most good actors. *(L)*

To Hugh Wheeler, on the final rehearsals
of his production of The Complaisant Lover:
The play is quite brilliant and the two men splendid –
only Phyllis Calvert is *un peu constipé* and overlaid. I
trust an audience will prise open her rather shuttered
technique. *(L)*

To Ruth and Augustus Goetz, after revisiting his production of their play The Heiress, *which starred Ralph Richardson and Peggy Ashcroft:*
I bullied Ralph a bit about his opening scene, and tried to persuade him not to pick Peggy's handkerchief at the party as if he were Fagin teaching the Artful Dodger. *(L)*

To Noël Coward, on the need to rehearse Michael Wilding, who had taken over his part in Nude with Violin*:*
His speech is a problem. Nothing can be done until he has played in for a couple of weeks, then I shall come down with my cohorts all gleaming and beat the fuck out of him. *(L)*

ॐ

Aware of his faults as a director, he was quick to point out his deficiencies as an actor.

To George Rylands, on his playing in his wartime season at the Haymarket:
Desmond McCarthy helped me a lot, especially about what our dear Allies call my tendency to become piss elegant. I am curbing my unfortunate tendency to 'hold the pose' and sit down with my knees together *à la* Marie Tempest. *(L)*

To Julian Glover, during rehearsals for The Tempest:
One thing you must never do is cry on stage. Of course I
always do, but then I'm so sweet.

To Jerome Kilty, who told him off for crying
during a performance of The Ides of March:
I can't help it. I was born with my bladder
too close to my eyes: one blink, and it comes out.

At a question and answer session
at the National Theatre after a performance of Tartuffe:
I'm terribly miscast. It should have been Charles Laughton
in the part, but he's dead. *(Joan Plowright)*

To George Rylands, in response to an anonymous
critic of his wartime Hamlet:
I painstakingly revise my diction with a tuning fork and a
pruning knife every two weeks or thereabouts. *(L)*

℃℈

*There were some unexpected moments
behind the scenes when he played Raskolnikov
in* Crime and Punishment *on Broadway.*

Glenn Jordan
He had an emotional confession scene in which he wept
copiously, while Marian Seldes, who was on stage listening
to him, also wept copiously. When they exited, he turned
to her and said: 'Remember Marian, *I* killed the old lady,
not *you*!'

On Audrey Fildes, who was playing Sonia:
She irritated me, so I came on from the other side just to
annoy her. (*Frith Banbury*)

ↄ

*He could be frank about his limitations
for certain Shakespearean roles.*

Explaining why he didn't want to play Malvolio in Twelfth Night*:*
I am quite unable to act without suggesting good breeding.
(Kenneth Tynan)

On his suitability for the title-role in Julius Caesar:
I don't think I'm a bit like Caesar really. They just think of someone with a big nose and a noble manner. *(U)*

2

Designers and Audiences

On playing Hamlet at 40:

'Thank God for paint when golden youth
is on the wane at last!'

*He had some idiosyncratic views about designers,
and was always highly conscious of the effect of
his costumes – and those of his fellow-actors.*

Alan Strachan
We were talking at a party about his forthcoming production of *The Gay Lord Quex*, and he said: 'Alan Tagg is a very clever designer, but all his sets seem to be round.'

To Frith Banbury:
I don't think Reece Pemberton is a good designer. You want someone who will just come in and do something red.

On taking over the role of Richard II from Paul Scofield for a performance in Southern Rhodesia:
I don't know how Paul coped with this costume; it's like an over-heavy hostess frock. *(Geoffrey Bayldon)*

To Michael Ayrton, on playing the title-role in his wartime production of Macbeth:
I have had my last tunic made longer, and abandoned the boots in favour of chain-mail, as Alan Dent says my knees are not suited to the exhibition of high tragedy, and I fancy he speaks some truth. *(L)*

To his mother, while playing Hamlet on tour during the war:
My clothes are very successful – also the new wig! Thank God for paint when golden youth is on the wane at last! *(L)*

To Christopher Fry, on his Othello at Stratford:
Zefferelli made the fatal mistake of dressing me as a Venetian, so that I looked, as many of the notices said, like an Indian civil servant. *(L)*

To George Devine, at the dress parade
for the Noguchi King Lear, *a production notorious*
for its weird costumes, Lear's being full of holes:
I'm terribly worried about this costume. I look like a gruyère cheese. *(Jeremy Burnham)*

To his mother, on his costume for Jason in Medea:
I am scrapping my first dress altogether as I look thoroughly obvious in it – like any classical general in *Antony and Cleopatra* or *Julius Caesar*, or as if I was going to sing *Tristan. (L)*

To Paul Anstee, on Irene Worth's appearance in Tiny Alice:
The negligee makes her look like Lady Dracula, and in the get-up for the last act, with a short skirt and hooded cloak, she looks like a Blue Cross nurse who has mislaid her collecting box. *(L)*

To Peggy Ashcroft, on the costumes for his Broadway Hamlet:
Malcolm Keen as Claudius has a very elaborate grey affair with lacy frills at the knees which look idiotic in the praying scene – he is like Charles II in a bad temper. *(L)*

Audiences both provoked and amused him, and he was famous for his ability while in full emotional flood to take in details of their appearance and behaviour.

To Robin Phillips, who suggested during rehearsals of Caesar and Cleopatra *that he was being too melodious:*
It's my audience, my adorable but bloody fans. They come for my voice, and I'm afraid not to give it to them.

To Michael Feast, on hearing a loud bravo during a curtain call for The Tempest*:*
I think the landlady must be in tonight.

To Ann Bell, on noticing a coach party arriving for a matinee of Veterans, *which starred screen idol John Mills, and contained a lot of swear words:*
They've come expecting to see Scott of the Antarctic, but all they'll get is this terrible language.

On a first-night audience in Toronto
for his production of Hamlet:
They'd only come to look at each other's frocks.
(Richard L Sterne)

To his mother, during the run of
Measure for Measure *at Stratford:*
Lord Pethick-Lawrence, who was in front on
Friday, was heard to ask in a loud voice, as the
lights went out on my first soliloquy:
'Was that Allen Quartermaine?'!! *(L)*

To his mother, on the Dublin opening of Nude with Violin:
It was a gala audience. The gallery rained paper darts on to
the footlights during the intervals, but it seems this was only
a display of native exuberance. *(L)*

To Frances Cuka, during the interval of Half-Life:
Did you see that woman in the front row in the purple dress
with the amethyst necklace and amethyst earrings to match,
and the man in the tuxedo next to her who fell asleep?

3

Portraits of the Artists

On playing King Lear:
'Get yourself a small Cordelia.'

He was a shrewd observer of others in his profession, and specialised in witty, sometimes scurrilous and occasionally cruel epithets about their work, character or behaviour.

To Richard Eyre, on Lilian Baylis:
She was an extraordinary old woman.
I don't think she knew her arse from her elbow. *(I)*

To Oliver Cotton, on Laurence Olivier:
He's rather a cold man, but he writes very good letters.

Paul Bogart
After I had seen *A Month in the Country* he asked me
what I thought of Michael Redgrave. 'Excellent,' I said.
'Bloody waxworks,' he muttered.

To Peter Shaffer, on Edith Evans:
The Christian Science was churning away inside of her like
an ill-made curry. Why is it that with Edith one says, 'Oh
how marvellous, how exciting to see her,' but within ten
minutes one says, 'Oh God! How do I leave this crushing
bore?!'

On Lindsay Anderson:
Quite a pleasant little man. Rather short, wore a funny cap. I
think gay, but not quite up to it. *(Richard Briers)*

On Ingrid Bergman:
Dear Ingrid, she speaks five languages
and can't act in any of them. *(S)*

*On Gladys Cooper, who had agreed to appear
in his production of* The Chalk Garden*:*
She won't know the words, but it won't matter,
because she'll just say whatever she likes. *(Judith Stott)*

To John Miller, on Laurence Olivier:
When I was rehearsing him as Malvolio in *Twelfth Night* he
was very set on playing the part in his own particular way,
which I thought was a little bit extravagant. He played it like
a Jewish hairdresser, with a great lisp. He would fall off a
bench in the garden scene, though I begged him not to. *(I)*

To Alan Schneider, on Edward Albee:
I saw him for a minute as he was passing
through London. I gather he has given up the grape.
He looked like a surly pirate with his
drooping moustache. *(L)*

To Brian Case, on Vanessa Redgrave
She's a marvellous actress, *and* she manages to find time
for all that political rubbish. *(I)*

To Tony Wharmby, after filming a scene of
Why Didn't They Ask Evans?, *during*
which Bernard Miles had frequently forgotten his lines:
I can't imagine why they made him a lord.
The fellow's simply not up to it.

To Paul Anstee, while rehearsing
Much Ado About Nothing *in America:*
Micheál MacLíammóir as Don Pedro in his Frankie
Howerd toupee a great joy. He looks a bit like Widow
Twankey and camps dreadfully. He blows kisses in the
air, fidgets and reacts, killing laughs in all directions.
Starring so long with bad companies in the bogs
of Ireland, he imagines he is bound to steal all the
thunder for himself. *(L)*

To Alec Guinness:
Martita Hunt is to be the Vicaress in *The Cradle Song*,
at which, like Christian, I rejoice and tremble – never,
surely, shall I persuade her to take the varnish off
those famous claws. *(L)*

To Leon Quartermaine, on a biography of
Harley Granville-Barker by CB Purdom:
Purdom is a horrid little knickerbockered know-all,
who never really knew HGB at all. *(L)*

To Cecil Beaton,
on his production of Lady Windermere's Fan*:*
Dorothy Hyson tweets more like a canary than ever.
Athene Seyler does one or two naughty mandarin nods
for fear the audience mightn't see the joke, and Isabel
Jeans' walk splays outwards with a strange totter that
suggests the cab horse about to slip on an icy paving
stone saving itself by a valiant effort. *(L)*

On Lewis Casson, after spotting him with
an over-made-up red mouth:
Here comes Uncle Hot Lips! *(John Moffatt)*

To Barbara Quartermaine, on Raymond Mander and
Joe Mitchenson, collectors of theatrical memorabilia:
They're a strange, freakish pair, dedicated collectors,
middle-aged, one rather dandified, the other with a
broken nose, looking like a Shaw burglar. *(L)*

To Paul Anstee, on Edith Evans
at the end of the run of Henry VIII*:*
Edith has been terribly Mrs Gummidge,
and I think was as delighted to go home
as we were to see the last of her. *(L)*

To Paul Anstee, on Leontyne Price:
We were very bored with *Aida* last night.
An incredibly vulgar production. Leontyne Price sang
beautifully, but acts like a barmaid serving
drinks to the cowboys! *(L)*

*To Cecil Beaton, after visiting his cousin
Edward Gordon Craig in the south of France:*
Craig was very picturesque – in a huge straw hat, a
sort of surgeon's white overall, with a turned-up collar
à la William Nicholson, and a white burnous thrown
over one shoulder and tucked across his lap, so that he
could adjust his truss at meal times with discretion.

To his mother, on the actor/director Arthur Bouchier:
I found him quite different
to what I expected – very intelligent – for an actor. *(L)*

To John Miller:
Orson Welles came over to play Moriarty in one episode of
a terrible Sherlock Holmes radio series Ralph Richardson
and I did. We went to lunch at the Etoile in Soho, and he
was so avuncular, he shouted and laughed so loud, the whole
restaurant started staring at us, and Ralph and I felt like two
little boys from Eton who had been taken out to lunch by a
benevolent uncle. *(I)*

*To his mother, after noticing the presence of two rival
theatre historians while he was playing Hamlet in Elsinore:*
Rosamond Gilder and Phyllis Hartnoll eye each other like two
angry codfish. *(L)*

> *To Paul Anstee, on Lillian Gish:*
> We saw a most undistinguished
> production of *Romeo and Juliet*.
> Juliet is only twenty-two but
> managed to look like Edith Sitwell.
> Lillian Gish impossible,
> alas, as the Nurse – Rebecca of
> Sunnybrook Farm with
> a dash of Mary Poppins. *(L)*

To his mother, while on holiday in the south of France:
Larry Olivier and Vivien Leigh come for a week,
and Jill Esmond for another – these ex-married couples
playing Box and Cox need much tact and discrimination
in the handling. *(L)*

To Hugh Wheeler, on Vivien Leigh:
Lady Viv is back in London with
a good many straws in her hair. *(L)*

> *To Lindsay Anderson, on Peggy Ashcroft:*
> She's never been good at getting her hair
> done, or spending money on dresses. *(D)*

To Hugh Wheeler, on Somerset Maugham:
They say old Willie is rather round the bend – all those injections have gone below the waist and the brain seems to have suffered. *(L)*

To his mother, on Marie Tempest, with whom
he was rehearsing Dear Octopus:
The play seems fairly well set now, and she seems sure of her lines, though not always the order in which they come. *(L)*

To Martita Hunt:
Martita dear, if you gather any more poise you'll fall over backwards. *(Leslie French)*

John Mortimer
He once said on television that
Peter Sellers had a face like an uncooked ham.

ɞ

He also liked to pass on his memories of famous writers.

*To Mark Amory, on meeting TS Eliot
to discuss a production of* The Family Reunion*:*
We had lunch at the Reform Club.
He was just like a civil servant, with striped trousers. *(I)*

To his mother, on meeting Thornton Wilder:
He is a funny little nervous man, like a dentist turned
professor – shy and suddenly incoherently explosive,
with expressive hands when he suddenly speaks of
something he knows about. *(L)*

To John Cornwell, on a memory of Evelyn Waugh:
I once knew Waugh. He came to see me at a rehearsal.
He affected an enormous ear trumpet, although
he wasn't at all deaf. He was very nice to me,
which surprised me, because he was supposed
to be very bitchy. *(I)*

To Lillian Gish, on Harold Pinter:
I have just met Pinter for the first time,
and he really is surprisingly nice. *(L)*

❧

He frequently made pithy or waspish remarks about his fellow-actors' performances, both in his own productions and others.

On Leon Quartermaine as Gloucester in King Lear*:*
His only concession to the storm was to fasten his top button. *(Timothy Bateson)*

To his mother, on Milton Rosmer, who was playing Macduff in his production of Macbeth*:*
Rosmer is back, but plays as if he was in the Whispering Gallery. *(L)*

To Paul Anstee, on the Claudius and Gertrude in his Broadway production of Hamlet*:*
Alfred Drake and Eileen Herlie seem like an ex-croupier from Monte Carlo who has eloped with a fat landlady, who keeps a discreet brothel on the Cote d'Azur. *(L)*

To Paul Anstee, after seeing Gigi *on Broadway:*
Hermione Gingold is very bad indeed, like an old Jewish wolf in drag. *(L)*

To Paul Anstee, after seeing a production of Macbeth *in Boston:*
Siobhan McKenna yelled as if she was in Marble Arch
in the sleepwalking scene, which she chose to play in a
flowing white Hollywood negligee which floated round the
stage like a Christmas angel. 'Callas Athene',
I christened her rather wickedly. *(L)*

To Hugh Wheeler, on Christopher Fry's new play:
Curtmantle is a crashing bore. Gwen Ffrangcon-Davies'
bracelets started to jangle early in the first act,
and I began winding up my watch, so no doubt the
actors found it hard to make themselves heard. *(L)*

To Vivien Leigh and Laurence Olivier, on the play Royal Circle*:*
Even Lilian Braithwaite, who staggered on occasionally like
a terrifying scarecrow, manages to waft a few faint laughs out
of the air. *(L)*

On Sybil Thorndike as Lady Macbeth:
Lewis Casson's production was clumsy and over-pictorial,
with Sybil looking like an over-dressed parrot. *(L)*

જ

Kenneth Tynan, who delivered several savage reviews of his performances, was not his favourite critic. But his real bête noire was his fellow-actor Donald Wolfit, whom he disliked for his arrogance, self-importance and pettiness.

To Stark Young:
Kenneth Tynan is a brilliant but rather odious young fellow, who is good when he is enthusiastic, but cheap and personal when he dislikes anyone's work (he hates mine). He is very good to read as long as it isn't you. *(L)*

To Richard Mangan, on Donald Wolfit:
While we were touring during the war,
we had to change trains at Crewe.
All the carriages were blacked out.
When I opened one door, there he was sitting inside.
I said: 'My God, it's the enemy!' and ran.

To John Mortimer, after reading a book about Lord Lucan:
Can you really get someone to do a murder for £3,000?
I suppose Donald Wolfit would have paid that to get
rid of me. He did hate me so. *(I)*

To Vivien Leigh, on hearing Wolfit had been 'torn to shreds' by the New York critics for his company's Shakespeare productions:
He has a bee in his knickers the like of which no onion will assuage. He must be incredibly cross, but I have not the slightest compunction in being delighted. *(L)*

To George Rylands:
How dare you, sir, presume to compare my art with those two posturing mountebanks Messrs Wolfit and Olivier? *(L)*

To his mother, while touring
The Importance of Being Earnest in Canada:
We have done a very fine week financially here in Montreal, and I'm glad to say we have beaten Wolfit's figure financially! *(L)*

To his mother, on how he avoided meeting Wolfit while they were both in Stratford:
Mr Wolfit wished to be photographed with me – Hamlets past and present – for the local press, but I was not to be drawn, and was in my bath! *(L)*

He was always happy to pass on the benefit of his experience to younger actors.

Michael Hordern
Before I had begun rehearsing as King Lear, he came round to my dressing-room. I asked him if he had any advice or help which might get me through the run. 'Yes,' he said. 'Get yourself a small Cordelia.' *(M)*

Gielgoodies:
The Man from Stratford

*Shakespeare was the dominant figure in his acting
and directing life. Not surprisingly, working
on his plays inspired some of his choicest remarks.*

Alec Guinness
During his season at the Queen's I was playing the small
part of the Groom in *Richard II*. At a last-minute rehearsal
just before the first night he said to me: 'You're not nearly as
good in the part as Leslie French was.' *(M)*

Tarquin Olivier
He was directing my father as Malvolio in *Twelfth Night*.
One day Larry was trying out a particular walk.
'Don't do that, Larry,' he said. 'It's so *vulgar*.'

Paul Scofield
That wonderfully comic actor George Rose was playing
Dogberry in his production of *Much Ado About Nothing*.
It was a brilliant creation. In the middle of one of
his scenes at the dress rehearsal John called out: 'Oh
George, George, do be *funny*!'

To Dorothy Tutin, cast as Hero, during rehearsals
for Much Ado About Nothing:
This scene is a terrible bore.
What can we do with Dorothy? Oh give her a fan.

To Alec Guinness, during a rehearsal for Hamlet:
Get someone to teach you how to act.
Try Martita Hunt – she'll be glad of the money. *(M)*

To Keith Michell, who was playing Orsino in Twelfth Night:
No, no, it's like Hotspur on a day off.

To William Devlin, playing Antonio,
during rehearsals of Twelfth Night:
Billy, can't you do something
more *interesting*? *(Michael Denison)*

To Jean Marsh, during rehearsals
for Much Ado About Nothing:
Hero, why are you walking
like a goosed policewoman?

To the cast of Henry VIII, *including Harry*
Andrews, reminiscing about his Hamlet in America:
I had a rather poor Horatio. Oh, it was you Harry. Well,
you've improved so much since then. *(I)*

To Trader Faulkner, during rehearsals
for Much Ado About Nothing:
For God's sake, Trader, stop swinging backwards and
forwards like a green baize door. You're not in vaudeville.

Lee Montague
During rehearsals for *Twelfth Night*
he passed me in the street, turned,
and said: 'Have we met?' I replied:
'Yes, I'm playing Fabian.' 'Oh yes,'
he said. 'An unmemorable part.'

To Jill Bennett,
during a rehearsal of Much Ado About Nothing:
You girl, move to the right. No, no, not *you*.
The ugly one with the big nose. *(John Moffatt)*

To Frith Banbury, during a rehearsal for Hamlet:
I can forgive you for being late, Banbury, but what I cannot
forgive is that you stand like that when you do arrive.

To Jeremy Burnham, who was wearing too much
make-up during a Shakespeare production:
Your face looks like Clapham Junction.

To Michael Malnick during a Shakespeare rehearsal at Stratford:
You're so tall, you're blocking everybody. Can't you be
shorter? *(Timothy West)*

During a technical rehearsal
for his wartime production of Macbeth*:*
Oh my God, you're all so *English*! *(Frank Thornton)*

During rehearsals for Hamlet,
in the hearing of the actor concerned:
It's such a pity one can never afford a really
good actor to play Fortinbras. *(Jonathan Cecil)*

John Moffatt
While he was rehearsing Dogberry and Verges in *Much
Ado About Nothing*, he said: 'I've no idea how to direct these
scenes, but I do know when you're not being funny.'

Michael Denison
At the start of the first reading of *Twelfth Night* at Stratford,
John said: 'I don't know what I've got to offer you in this
beautiful play, so let's see what *you* can offer *me*. We'll begin
and we'll read it without a break. Keith Michell as Orsino,
commence.' So Keith cleared his throat and said: 'If music'
– and John said: 'No, no, no, if *music*!' Two days later the
reading was completed.

ഗ

There were also moments to cherish in the wings.

To Geoffrey Bayldon, during a performance of King Lear, *when asked why he was not waiting to enter from his usual position:*
Alan Badel is over there and he keeps giving me notes.

To Doreen Aris, playing Miranda to his Prospero in The Tempest:
A friend has said I'm not fatherly enough,
so you'll find me more fatherly tonight.

John Standing
During one Shakespeare production Hazel Terry,
who was an alcoholic, had been smoking in her
dressing-room and had set fire to her costume. As she
wandered on to the stage with her train still on fire,
Gielgud observed from the wings: 'I see cousin Hazel
is alight again.'

About to lift up Peggy Ashcroft as the dead
Cordelia during a performance of King Lear:
Oh God, I wish I'd never taken up the bloody classics. *(S)*

Jeremy Burnham

During a performance of *King Lear* he was waiting to go on for the reconciliation scene with Cordelia, and suddenly came out with this limerick:

> There was a young lady of Barking Creek
> Who had her monthlies twice a week.
> A young man from Woking
> Said 'How very provoking.
> Not much time for poking,
> So to speak.

എ

But he behaved no less tactlessly in other offstage surroundings.

To John Miller:

My first meeting with Orson Welles was in London, when we were going down for the weekend to stay with the Oliviers. I said: 'What are you going to do here?' He replied: 'I'm going to play Othello.' And I said: 'On the *stage*? In *London*?' He wasn't very pleased. *(I)*

Donald Sinden
In *Much Ado About Nothing* at Stratford I was playing
Benedick and Judi Dench was Beatrice. Over lunch
at the Garrick I said to him: 'When I saw you playing
Benedick and Peggy Ashcroft was Beatrice, you
persuaded me that Benedick was a very witty fellow.
But now Judi and I have been taking the play apart in
rehearsal, and we think that Beatrice is the one with the
wit, and Benedick has the bar-room humour. 'You're
perfectly right, I made a great mistake,' he replied.
'Benedick is a very boorish fellow. You'll be much
better than I was.'

To Kenneth Branagh:
You're doing *Coriolanus*? I hate the play.
At *Chichester*? Nasty theatre. *(U)*

Peter Brook
During a few early performances of my production of *The
Winter's Tale* the understudy Frances Hyland had to go
on for Virginia McKenna. I got a call from HM Tennent
saying John thought she was an absolute disaster. I went to
a performance, and she was very good. Afterwards I said to
John: 'But she's marvellous, just perfect.' He said: 'I quite
agree, she's absolutely right.' 'But John, I got a message to
say you thought she was terrible.' 'It's true, I did say that,' he
said, 'but I hadn't looked.'

To Brian Bedford during the run of The Tempest,
in which Bedford was playing Ariel:
I met a man in the Burlington Arcade today.
He thought you were really quite good. *(U)*

To Orson Welles, during the filming of Chimes at Midnight*:*
Have you ever known an American who could play
Shakespeare? Oh, sorry, Orson. Well, I always thought you
were Irish. Or something. *(Keith Baxter)*

4

The Play's the Thing

'I've got my toe in the avant-garde.'

He never really took to Ibsen and Shaw, but Chekhov remained his favourite writer after Shakespeare.

To Noël Coward, while on tour in Norway:
Here in Oslo there is a very disagreeable smell in the theatre, which I thought was probably Ibsen's unpublished plays. *(L)*

To his mother, while playing in Ibsen's John Gabriel Borkman*:*
Erhart Borkman is a pill – but I've an effective bit, though he's an odious little cad – such a dreadful bunch of people anyway. *(L)*

To his mother, after seeing Ibsen's The Wild Duck*:*
A fine though to me revolting play. *(L)*

To his mother, after seeing Shaw's The Doctor's Dilemma*:*
Fine writing and brilliant dialogue, but too much of the usual Shavian impersonality and moralising for me. The human touch – if that's what it's called – more lacking than usual in this play. *(L)*

To Paul Anstee, after finishing with his production of Chekhov's Ivanov:
We've now played it in every size and medium except on ice or through glass, which I think would surprise the dear author if he could only see it. *(L)*

⌖

Late in his career he appeared in the work of modern playwrights, and enjoyed a new lease of life.

To Lillian Gish, on appearing in
The Ides of March *by Thornton Wilder:*
I've got my toe in the avant-garde,
just paddling around, not yet up to my knee. *(L)*

Robin Phillips
While we were discussing the designs for *Caesar and Cleopatra*, he said: 'I've been asked to do this new play *Home* by David Storey, but I'm really not sure about it. Both characters are quite mad, which is fine. I mean Ralph Richardson and I are completely cuckoo, so in that sense it's perfect casting. But oh dear. It's a sort of plaid shirt and cardigan play, with British summer sandals and nylon socks. I don't think I could bear to wear socks *and* sandals, not even for the Royal Court.'

To John Theocharis, on his anxiety about
working in Home *at the Royal Court:*
Ralph and I thought we would be terribly sent up by
all those left-wing boys in pigtails, sitting in their blue
jeans reading pamphlets on the staircase. But they
were so kind, they couldn't have worked harder at the
Haymarket. *(L)*

To Alan Bennett, who during rehearsals of Forty Years On *had*
declined his suggestion that he write a Coward parody for the
second act:
Why not? It's terribly easy. Noël does it all the time. *(M)*

To Alan Bennett, complaining about the play's opening:
All that terrible organ music, the slow march
and the hymns. Oh those hymns, it's just like school.
Bennett But it *is* school.
Gielgud Yes I suppose it is. *(M)*

To John Theocharis,
on Peter Brook's rehearsal exercises for Oedipus*:*
It was like being in the army. I felt it was my punishment for
not going to the war. *(L)*

To Peter Shaffer, after being cast in his play The Shrivings:
Have you thought of Ralph for the other part?
He's a natural rapist.

On his role in Charles Wood's play Veterans:
I knew it was based on me.
I think I made myself rather a dear. *(Frances Cuka)*

To John Miller
Ralph Richardson and I said we were becoming like the broker's men in *Cinderella*, doing these double acts in *Home* and *No Man's Land*. *(I)*

❧

The roles that appealed to him were not always predictable.

Christopher Miles:
While he was appearing as a valet in Coward's *Nude with Violin* I asked him what part he'd most like to play. He said: 'A serial killer in Brighton.'

❧

He was thoroughly unsympathetic to some
of the new trends in theatre.

Anna Carteret
During rehearsals for *Oedipus* with Peter Brook directing we
would explore various themes. One day it was Shock. Each of
us had to say the most shocking thing we could think of, such
as necrophilia, and so on. When it was John's turn he said as
quick as a flash: 'We open in two weeks' time.'

To Ralph Richardson,
who had been offered Beckett's Waiting for Godot*:*
It's a load of old rubbish. *(B)*

Bill Gaskill
George Devine tried to persuade him to
join the Royal Court, and to play in
Beckett's *Endgame*. He said: 'I couldn't bear
to play it, to say all those things in public.'

On stage nudity:
The young avant-garde theatre doesn't use make-up at all.
They want to take their clothes off, which isn't quite the same
thing. *(L)*

To Cecil Beaton, on Joe Orton's What the Butler Saw*:*
They send me things I don't understand. This new Joe Orton
play for example. All the cast say the most awful things to
one another. I wouldn't touch it. *(L)*

Peter Gill
I was asked to direct a play by Robert Shaw.
I went to see John about it. 'Why would I want to do
this?' he said. 'There's no scene with the leading woman,
and all the leading characters have just
been hanged.'

Frith Banbury
He was watching a play by David Mercer, in which the actors
came among the audience. One of them had chosen John,
who explained: 'I told her to bugger off. I thought it was in
the spirit of the piece.'

To Cecil Beaton, on the new generation of actors:
Their skin is in such a bad condition, David Hemmings and
the like. All covered in spots and boils. But they don't seem
to mind, and they have a great success with girls.

He was also scornfully dismissive of the new National
Theatre building on the South Bank.

To Glen Byam Shaw:
Oh God, what a soul-destroying edifice – nay,
factory. Like a badly run nursing home. *(L)*

To Victor Davis:
The National is like an airport.
And all those corridors and doors to open. *(I)*

To Michael Owen:
The National Theatre is just so huge now, and so is the
Royal Shakespeare Company. Must they do all these
plays? The poor actors must get so tired. *(I)*

5

Words, Words, Words

'The quality of Mersey is not strained.'

*He had a great feel for and sensitivity to language,
and a constant delight in making puns.*

Irene Worth
At the dress rehearsal of *Oedipus*, we were discussing the height of a spike on which as Jocasta I had to impale myself. I suggested we might need a plinth. John called out from the wings, falling about with laughter: 'Plinth Philip or Plinth Charles?' *(I)*

Denis Quilley
We had one scene together in *Murder on the Orient Express*. I had to ask him what book he was reading, and when he told me I had to say: 'Is it about sex?' And he said: 'Wouldn't it be funny if I looked at my watch and said: "No, it's about half-past seven!"' The director Sidney Lumet roared with laughter, and said: 'Put that in.'

Bill Hays
After a meal in a restaurant in Ireland we went to the gents. The Bishop of Kerry was in the middle stall of the urinals. I was a little drunk, and after he left I said: 'That was a bishop prick.' Straight away John replied: 'We call it a diocese now.'

To Paul Herzberg
'You should stage a South African musical on Broadway, and call it *Assegais and Dolls*.' *(L)*

Richard Mangan
For the blinding of Oedipus he used eye patches, so as one of the stage managers I had to guide him on to the stage. Later, when I asked him to sign a copy of his book *Early Stages*, he wrote in it: 'The Eyes Have It.'

To Paul Anstee, while playing the spokesman for the High Lama of Shangri-La in the musical re-make of Lost Horizon: The film is going to cost six million dollars, so let's hope the music will be the making of it – nothing else will! I have christened it 'Hello, Dalai!' *(L)*

To Emlyn Williams and company while rehearsing his play Spring, 1600, *after being informed that Edna Best had suddenly left for America to join her husband Hebert Marshall, who had an artificial leg:*
I did hear Bert has been a bit footloose in Hollywood. *(M)*

Peter Brook
At the first costume rehearsal for *Venice Preserv'd*, John looked at all the women wearing long dresses, and said: 'I suppose I'm the man who watches trains go by.'

Discussing the famous line 'Kill Claudio!'
in Much Ado About Nothing*:*
My great-aunt Ellen Terry used to say
that if you don't get a laugh there,
the play becomes Much Ado
About *Something*. *(Timothy Bateson)*

After observing the auditions requiring actors
to appear naked in the film of Julius Caesar*:*
Buttocks wouldn't melt in their mouths. *(L)*

On filming Eagle in a Cage *in Yugoslavia,*
where two horses had thrown their riders:
I've decided to call them the Bolting Brothers. *(L)*

To Emlyn Williams, discussing his play Spring, 1600*:*
Let's call it *Whores for Tennis*. There's Angela, she wouldn't
play it Baddeley, but Edna might be Best. *(M)*

To Paul Anstee, on the Broadway theatre scene:
A big musical called *Ari* opened to a disastrous press.
They are *not* wild about *Ari*! *(L)*

Jeremy Burnham
Moira Lister had been commissioned to write a column for the *Daily Mail* about the Stratford Shakespeare company's European tour. But her piece about Berlin was censored for political reasons. When someone told John this, he said: 'She's got Reuters' cramp.'

To Paul Anstee:
How I loved Patrick Woodcock's joke about the Simone Signoret *Macbeth* at the Royal Court: 'Aimez-vous Glamis?' *(L)*

To James Agate:
There was a very nice misprint in the *Liverpool Echo* on Wednesday, paying tribute to our broad comedian George Woodbridge, who plays the Porter in *Macbeth*, as 'an engaging Portia'. I could not forbear to murmur that the quality of Mersey is not strained. *(L)*

On having to climb a steep hill while filming
Eagle in a Cage:
I think the film should be re-named
Climb and Punishment. (L)

Daniel Thorndike
John Bury had done a design incorporating juddering rocks for the transformation scene in *The Tempest*. During the technical rehearsal John exclaimed: 'It's the Rocky Horror Show!'

Lee Montague
During the filming of *Eagle in a Cage* I had to ride a big horse high up on the battlements. I was sick with fear. John was watching, and said to me afterwards: 'I hope they show the film in black and white, because you were looking very green.'

John Mortimer
We were driving along in France behind a great big pile of wood on a lorry, and he started to giggle, and I said: 'What is it?' And he replied: 'I just wonder where the nigger is in that woodpile.'

To his mother, after reading scenes from Hamlet
with the Old Vic company at Harrow School:
We were very pleased at pushing *fortissimo* in all the bawdy lines which had been removed from the school edition. Can you imagine, 'vixenlike' for 'like a whore'!!! *(L)*

Tarquin Olivier
He and Vivien Leigh often did the *Times* crossword together. He was very quick. Once I was travelling in a car with them, and one clue was: 'A red herring who proposes easily.' Straight away he said: 'Ginger pop.'

Shakespeare quotations stood him in good stead in certain circumstances.

Cordelia Monsey
At the dress rehearsal of Peter Hall's production of *The Tempest* he walked towards the trapdoor – and suddenly disappeared. Peter went completely white. Nobody dared to venture on to the stage. Eventually he emerged unscathed, saying: 'Oh that this too, too solid flesh would melt.'

Charles Wood
While we were filming *The Charge of the Light Brigade* in Turkey, we all went out on a yacht he had rented. One of the crew caught a fish for lunch, and as it splashed into the pan John remarked: 'Alas! Poor mullet, I knew him well.'

He delighted in re-telling stories and jokes
he had heard. Some came at unexpected moments,
while many were decidedly naughty.

To John Miller
I remember hearing from Alan Webb, who was in a film with
Lassie. Each day they used to bring an entire wagon full of
Lassies to the studio – the smiling Lassie, the scowling Lassie,
the mordant Lassie – and there was a great argument when
they won the Academy Award about which one should be
chosen to sit in the chair at the dinner. *(I)*

To fellow-actors, while waiting for his cue
during the wartime Hamlet:
A Home Guard soldier had been ordered to disguise himself
as a tree. He had been so successful that he was mistaken
for the real thing by the local flora and fauna. 'I didn't mind
the birds searching for insects,' he said. 'But when a pair of
squirrels started looking for any nuts I thought the whole
exercise had gone too far.'
(Richard Johnson)

To Paul Anstee:
A Bobby Lewis joke.
Do you know what a circumcised cock looks like?
Yul Brynner in a turtle-necked sweater. *(L)*

To Hugh Wheeler:
A good story for you. Harold Hobson, fancying himself
no end in the French, insists on being the only London
journalist to interview Jean Genet when he comes over for
The Balcony. On arriving at Genet's hotel, silence ensues for
some minutes, and Hobson's completely gravelled for an
opening. Genet (breaking silence suddenly): '*Donc! Vous êtes
pédéraste?*' Hobson (leaping for cover): '*Non, monsieur, je suis
critique!*' *(L)*

To Paul Anstee:
Ben-Gurion cabled to the Pope:
'Cancel Easter, we've found the body.' *(L)*

To Irene Worth:

Two nice anecdotes about Ingrid Bergman in *The Constant Wife*. She said to Barbara Ferris one night in the last act: 'I like you. I think you are a cheat, a liar and a hamburger – but I like you.' And once she asked Dorothy Reynolds why she had lost a good laugh she had been used to getting. Dorothy said: 'I think if you turned your face to the audience, you would get the laugh.' Ingrid cast her eyes to heaven and remarked: 'All these *rules*!'*(L)*

To Paul Anstee:

I'm reading Barbara Tuchman's *The Proud Tower*. Divine story in it of Wilde meeting a terrible bore, who said: 'You know, Wilde, I feel there is a conspiracy of silence against me these days. What do you think I ought to do about it?' 'Join it,' said Oscar. *(L)*

To Alan Bennett, on the hostess Emerald Cunard, who had summoned him to dine at the Dorchester during the Blitz:
She surveyed the table and rang for the waiter. 'Where is the butter?' 'There is no butter, ma'am.' 'No butter! But what is the merchant navy doing?'

❦

He liked to entertain his friends
with the occasional literary offering.

To Glen Byam Shaw, sending him lines written
after the first night of King Lear *at Stratford:*
Our heart belongs to Daddy, BUT
Don't ask Daddy to stay.
His knights are the devil to pay.
His boat hath a leak,
And he dared not speak,
And he's started to butter his hay!
(L)

To Irene Worth,
thanking her for a birthday present of flowers:
Dearest Eliza,
Your patch at Covent Garden must have been bereft
yesterday, for my house is blooming wonderful with glorious
colours and stripes in every hue. So loving and thoughtful
– thank you. Don't forget our English lesson on Sunday.
Fondly, H Higgins. *(L)*

To Julian Randall
The March of Time (1911-1946),
Issued by The Trouser Press, Cock Yard, Cripplegate, E.C.
Development (not yet arrested), or *Plus corduroyiste que le roi*

At school I loved to watch, with furtive greed,
Young masters part their coats of Harris Tweed,
Jingling and thrusting in their trouser pockets,
While youthful eyes popped from their pupils' sockets.
Grey flannels were the then prevailing fashion,
And for these garments I conceived a passion.
Masters and boys, in tempting shades of greys,
Disturbed my nights and dramatised my days.

The First Great War was quite an education,
In uniform and mutual masturbation,
In riding breeches, boots and spurs, peaked caps,
And streamlined whipcords bulging at the flaps.
The Twenties blossomed – boys in peacock hues,
Whose Oxford trousers quite concealed their shoes,
Fawn, pink, cerise, in serge or gabardine,
The hearty looked as garish as the queen.

The Thirties ushered in a compromise,
Discreet zip-fasteners took the place of flies.
The width decreased, but looseness still remained,
And corduroys were Paradise Regained.
Breeches, alas, now shunned by the nobility,
Resumed a strict equestrian utility.
Plus-fours waxed gross in hideous baggy tiers,
And velvet vanished with the Cavaliers.
Grey flannels, shaved in worsted, off the peg,
Lost all distinction on the common leg.

Then, in the Second War's most hideous year,
With siren suits for every wear and tear,
With women breeched in shameless imitation,
And blackout time the crudest compensation,
The gloomy curtain rose an inch or so,
Official sanction played the gigolo.
Austerity decreed that men and boys
Should help the war by wearing corduroys.
The British citizens complied with pleasure,
Gave their five coupons, donned for work and leisure,
Squeaking and rustling, grey and pink and brown,
Creased for the country, pressed and washed for town.
The Desert Rats took them for battle dress,
And Monty's 'cords' made headlines in the Press,
When suddenly, without a word of warning,
Once more the knell to masculine adorning.
The government announced in accents cultural,
'No corduroy, save for the Agricultural.'

Prince, you and I have noted predilections,
Britons shall not be slaves to such restrictions.
We'll crave indulgence, by the country's pardon,
Dress in fresh cords and cultivate our garden. *(L)*

Gielgoodies:
Rehearsals and Auditions

In rehearsals his wounding remarks were often about the appearance, size or manner of members of the cast. Many of his sharpest arrows were aimed at actresses.

To Maggie Smith, during a rehearsal of Private Lives*:*
Don't screw your face up like that, Maggie. You look like that terrible old woman you played in that dreadful film. Oh no, I didn't mean *Travels with My Aunt*. (S)

Siân Phillips
During the dress parade for *The Gay Lord Quex* Judi Dench came on in a dressing gown expressly made not to fit, as the plot required. John cried out: 'Oh God, no, Judi! You look just like Richard the Third!'

To Robert Flemying, during a rehearsal for Love for Love:
You look so ghastly at the back.
Do come forward. *(Derek Granger)*

To Sandra Dorne, while rehearsing Treasure Hunt:
You point too much, you have too big fingers.
(Terence Longdon)

Tom Rand
During rehearsals for *The School for Scandal* he walked down
the aisle and said to Pinkie Johnstone: 'Why is it, darling,
that when you come on the whole play falls flat?'

*To Trader Faulkner, who was understudying Richard
Burton, while rehearsing* The Lady's Not for Burning:
Oh dear, Richard had such a beautiful smile. You have
the most unfortunate crooked teeth. You really should
have something done to straighten them.

To Terence Longdon, during rehearsals for Treasure Hunt:
You drop your voice at the end of a sentence. You're too like
Roger Livesey.

To Martin Jarvis, during a rehearsal for the stage recital of
Paradise Lost, *in which he acted as Milton the narrator:*
It's all wrong, you know. I shouldn't be *reading*.
Milton was *blind*. *(M)*

Benjamin Whitrow:
When we were rehearsing *The School for Scandal*
he said to one actor: 'That's very glib. Have you done
a lot of weekly rep?'

To Siân Phillips, during a rehearsal of The Gay Lord Quex*:*
You must sit: you're so terribly tall when you're standing up.

Tom Rand
He once said to a cast who had given him
a first-night present: 'I knew you were too nice a
company to be any good.'

ᘒ

Rehearsals for his opera productions brought forth several classic remarks.

Jonathan Miller
While he was directing a production of *Don Giovanni* for the English National Opera there was an orchestral rehearsal, which meant the conductor was in charge. When they came to the sextet, he wanted to make a change. He ran down the aisle, shouting to the conductor: 'Do stop that *ghastly* music!'

Dulcie Gray
He had invited me to a dress rehearsal of *The Trojans*, which he was directing at Covent Garden. When the Trojan Horse came on he said to the Chorus: 'No! No! No! That won't do at all. You're supposed to be full of emotion, you're frightened, you're excited, you've never seen anything like it.' They did it several times, and then he gave them a long spiel about the various emotions they should have. 'One last time,' he said. But again they showed almost no emotion, so he rushed down from the back of the stalls, saying: 'No, no, no, you look as if you're seeing some not very good friends off from Waterloo station'

To John Copley, during one of the purely
processional scenes in The Trojans*:*
Can't we cut some of this terrible silent music?

To Dudley Jones, a very short Welsh actor, who had asked
him whether the singers in The Trojans *had been good actors:*
Some of them had a real flair for it – apart from the chorus,
which was full of Welsh dwarves. *(Robert Vahey)*

To John Copley, commenting on the music which Britten had
written for the rude mechanicals in A Midsummer Night's
Dream *at Covent Garden:*
Why did he write this dreadful music for these
beautiful words?

❧

Auditions, when actors are often
at their most vulnerable and insecure, were also the
occasion for some spectacular gaffes.

Jonathan Cecil
I was auditioning for the part of a scoutmaster in *Halfway Up*
the Tree. He said: 'We've seen an awful lot of young actors,
and they've been awfully amusing. The trouble is, they
would always have to *pretend* to be ridiculous, whereas you'
– and then he tailed off.

When it was my turn in the auditions for *Richard II*, he said
to me: 'We have two very beautiful men playing Bushy and
Bagot. You might make a good contrast.'

*To Clive Francis, after he was recalled
for a second audition for* Halfway Up the Tree*:*
Oh God, no. No, no, no. I'm more than certain
I didn't ask for you back again.

Trader Faulkner
After my audition for *The Lady's Not for Burning*, he came
forward from the stalls to the footlights. 'What's your name?'
he said. 'Ronald Faulkner,' I replied. 'Ronald! God, what
a *dreary* name!' So I said: 'In Australia I'm known by my
nickname, Trader.' And he replied; 'Trader! What a *wonderful*
name. We'll bill you on Broadway as Trader.'

❦

During his early career it was the custom
after the first night for the leading actor to make
a curtain speech. He used such occasions to drop
some of his more celebrated bricks.

After the opening night in Brighton
of his production of The Way of the World*:*
I promise you, ladies and gentlemen, it will be much better
in London. *(Dilys Hamlett)*

To John Miller:
I was directing *The Merchant of Venice* at the Old Vic, but only
gave six rehearsals, as I was also busy filming. So Harcourt
Williams did most of the job. After the first night I came on
and said: 'I want to pay tribute to Harcourt Williams, who
has done most of the donkey-work.'*(I)*

After the opening of his production of
Romeo and Juliet, *while holding Edith Evans*
and Peggy Ashcroft by the hand:
Two leading ladies, the like of whom
I hope I shall never meet again.*(S)*

Jack Hawkins
The production of *Richard of Bordeaux* had reached its first anniversary. After the performance John stepped forward, thanked the audience for its support, and said: 'I know many of you have been to see us thirty or forty times.' He paused, and looked along the line of the cast, searching for words. His eyes lighted on me, and he added: 'In spite of changes in the cast.' *(M)*

After a wartime performance at the Old Vic of The Tempest,
for which Jessica Tandy had been replaced by Peggy Ashcroft:
Ladies and gentlemen, I know you will rejoice with all of us in relief at the news just received: Jessica Tandy is safely in America. *(S)*

*To his mother, on his curtain speech
in Manchester, while touring* Dear Brutus:
I said in my speech last night, 'I'm sorry to see your beautiful city laid waste,' and got the biggest laugh of the evening! One of the papers today said it was the first time anyone had called Manchester a beautiful city since the eighteenth century! *(L)*

To Hugh Wheeler, after the opening night in Liverpool
of Enid Bagnold's dreadful play The Last Joke:
I made a short speech ending:
'Thank you for your enthusiasm and *sympathy*.'
Fortunately Enid did not notice. *(L)*

༄

The gaffes continued during a tour of the Far East,
where he played Hamlet to the troops.

To an audience in Saigon:
I'd like to thank my company, and particularly the ladies,
who have travelled so many thousands of miles to give you
all so much pleasure. *(Nancy Nevinson)*

To an audience in India:
I'm very proud to be the general of this ship.
(Nancy Nevinson)

6

Gay Times

On playing Benedick in *Much Ado About Nothing*:
'I have trouble with warriors.'

As a gay man in a period when homosexual acts were illegal in Britain, he chose to keep his private life as private as possible, telling Simon Callow: 'I do admire people like you and Ian McKellen for coming out, but I can't be doing with that myself.' But his letters and remarks on the subject were often spiced with wit, and within his own world he was not at all reticent about being gay.

To Richard Addinsell:
I wish you had heard Mr Justice Langton, who finished his eulogy of my character by saying: 'I understand Mr Gielgud is still unmarried.' (Dramatic pause while everyone looked uncomfortable.) 'May I hope that he will soon meet with not only a Good Nymph but a Constant Companion.' La, la, Sir Percy. *(L)*

To Hubbell Pierce, on his arrest for cottaging:
I can't really bring myself to write about it, but it will make a nice three-volume novel to work at in the Old Actresses' Home when I am wheeled in there, in a few years' time, crippled, dusty and, no doubt, still leaning trouserwards to the end. *(L)*

Kitty Black

He was reading *Brideshead Revisited* for an audio tape. When he got to the death of Lord Marchmain he was in tears. Afterwards at lunch he said: 'I was very ashamed, I cry at everything. I cry for trumpets, I cry for queens – oh dear, perhaps I shouldn't have said that.'

Julian Glover
After the first night of *The Ides of March* in Brighton we were going out to have supper. John and Pinkie Johnstone and John Stride were walking, while I drove my car slowly alongside them. John turned to Pinkie and said: 'Julian looks as if he's trying to pick someone up. If he tried to pick *me* up, I would yield gracefully, as usual.'

While we were on tour in Oxford we were walking down to
the Playhouse in Beaumont Street, and he looked up at St
John's College and said: 'I once had one of the dons in that
room before lunch!'

*To Hugh Wheeler, who was staying
with Christopher Isherwood in San Francisco:*
I hope you are enjoying the California
Poppies and Mandragola, and that you have
not heard mysterious music in the night proceeding
from a musical box of strangely phallic shape and
design stuffed nicely down the front of a pair
of Christopher's silver grey flannel trousers, with
an antique key sticking out of the fly! *(L)*

Robin Hawdon
On tour with *The Last Joke*, while we were waiting to go on
stage, he said to me: 'Would you like to have dinner with
me after the show?' In fear and trepidation (he had recently
been prosecuted for his homosexual activities) I said: 'Thank
you, Sir John, that's very kind of you.' There was a pause,
then with a twinkle he added: 'Don't worry, Hazel Terry will
be along to chaperone us.'

George Baker
When he was performing *Ages of Man* in New York, we used to eat in the same restaurant. One night he turned up after leaving a party early, telling me: 'They had invited so many dazzling young things, my heart was like a humming-bird, it didn't know where to settle.'

Richard Mangan
He and Kenneth Tynan were at Binkie Beaumont's country house for the weekend. He was taking a pre-dinner stroll round the garden when he came across Tynan reading a book, and asked him what it was. Tynan, who had a stammer, replied: 'It's a b-b-book set in Alabama about a young man who gets himself thrown into prison so that he can be b-b-buggered by big black men!' 'Oh,' he said, 'can't quarrel with that!'

John Theocharis
We were having lunch in the BBC studio canteen when two young chaps in leather gear and reddish berets came in. 'How wonderful,' he said.' We're being invaded by pirates!'

To Paul Anstee, on his penchant for corduroy trousers:
I hope I shan't go completely dotty in the next five years and get put away in a Corduroy Concentration Camp for my last remaining time on earth. *(L)*

To Hugh Wheeler:
The National Gallery is so packed with shorts,
lederhosen, corduroy and other distracting
gentlemanly attributes that one is tempted to spend
long hours there – almost the only place in London
with air conditioning too – and there are always
the pictures! *(L)*

To Hugh Wheeler,
while planning a holiday with him in Italy:
In Florence there's Harold Acton and
Mr Berenson if we wish to re-enter
intellectual society for a day or two,
and I hear that Baron Paulo Langham
in Rome is liable to lay on Fabulous
Footmen and the Papal Guard at the
dinner table at the drop of a hat. *(L)*

Ian Bannen
We were filming a scene in *Gandhi* in the Directors' Club.
There were gigantic portraits on the wall, of Victoria and the
young Albert. John said: 'Such a lovely little waist he's got.'

Michael Craig

He was directing one of the Shakespeare history plays, in which a messenger had to bring on urgent news. John suggested he kneel and pray first. The actor didn't feel this was right because of the urgency of the news, and asked John why he wanted him to pray. John replied: 'You look so pretty on your knees.'

Martin Jenkins

I phoned him to ask if he would record the linking Chorus in *The Winter's Tale* for a radio production. He replied: 'Will the little boy in the tight white jeans be doing the "spot"?' I said I could arrange that. So he said: 'Then I'll do it.'

To Vivien Leigh, as he prepared to sail to America:
I hear Noël and Sam Behrman will both be on the *Queen Elizabeth*, so I shall have to see you on the QT. Who will be the first to make a pass at Stringer Davis and goose Jean Cadell? *(L)*

To Mark Amory, talking of Much Ado About Nothing*:*
Benedick should be a tough old army nut. I have trouble
with warriors. *(I)*

To Martin Jenkins:
My brother Val compensated
for me in the other direction
by having five wives, not to
mention numerous mistresses.

Nigel Jeffcoat
He was on location in New York, and strolling
down Fifth Avenue one lunch time. He was crossing
at a set of traffic lights when he dropped his neatly
furled umbrella. A traffic cop retrieved it, and called
out to him: 'Hey! Fairy! You dropped your wand.'
He received the umbrella back with a graceful nod,
twirled it elegantly towards the cop, and said: 'Vanish!'

7

In Front of the Camera

Rehearsing *Summer's Lease*:
'You want the old queen coming out of
the closet, do you?'

*He worked extensively in films and television
in his later years, often without caring too much about the
kind of roles he played, as long as they paid well.*

To Anthony Hopkins:
I'm going to Budapest to do a film. I don't know what the part is, but they tell me it's awfully good. *(L)*

To Irene Worth, about appearing as a butler
in the Roald Dahl story Neck:
I do my *Orient Express* performance again,
and begin to feel a bit like Alan Webb, who asks:
'Which of my six old men do you want this time?' *(L)*

To George Pitcher and Ed Cone,
on filming Molly Keane's Time After Time:
In one scene I had to act with thirteen cats,
three dogs, and a piglet wrapped in a towel.
There's glory for you. *(L)*

To Hugh Wheeler:
I gave a (highly truncated) Ghost in Richard Chamberlain's
TV *Hamlet* – done *à la* Monk Lewis in 1820s costume – I
looked like Napoleon at Ascot. *(L)*

To John Gorrie, on being cast as the preacher
in Portrait of the Artist as a Young Man:
I have to give an eight-page sermon
on the terrors of hell. Well, it's a good
thing to know the worst, I suppose. *(L)*

To George Pitcher and Ed Cone,
on preparing to film Arthur:
The picture is a bit common,
it seems to me, trying, but
not succeeding, to be a kind of
Woody Allen fantasy. *(L)*

To Irene Worth, after turning down
a part in Franco Zeffirelli's
TV mini-series Christ:
Everyone seems to be in it,
but the script of the bits I saw
didn't read very inspiringly,
except for the quotes from
you know who. *(L)*

ↂ

He worked in Hollywood on the film of Julius Caesar,
in which he played Cassius.

To Laurence Olivier and Vivien Leigh:
James Mason still talks through his nose, and Marlon
Brando looks as if he is searching for a baseball bat to beat
out his brains with. *(L)*

To his mother:
I am growing my beard for the end, and look like a
burglar or the thirteenth Apostle. The tent scene came
off pretty well, though I blink and fidget still in close-
ups, and my eyes wander as if I was looking to see if a
policeman was coming to arrest me. *(L)*

தை

*His relations with his directors were usually
extremely positive – with exceptions.*

Martyn Friend
I was directing him in a period detective film for a television
series. One day he plucked my sleeve between set-ups. 'This
script,' he said, 'it's awful shit, isn't it?' 'Yes John, it is.'
'Good. Just as long as we agree.'

While we were filming *Camille* he did a close-up shot two or three times, and then said to the director Desmond Davis: 'Not too much face acting, was there?'

To Hugh Wheeler, after appearing in a cameo role in The Wicked Lady*:*
The director Michael Winner is a mad nut. George Cukor, Harpo Marx and Lionel Bart rolled into one. *(L)*

To Albert Finney, who asked him who had directed him in Arthur on the Rocks, *the sequel to* Arthur*:*
I don't know, I never took him in. *(Ronald Harwood)*

༒

There were many other characteristic moments during his days of filming.

Nancy Nevinson
He was on horseback filming *The Charge of the Light Brigade* in Turkey. The director Tony Richardson twice gave him the signal to move forward, but when nothing happened, he asked John if he understood the instruction. '*I* understand it perfectly,' he replied, 'but does the horse?'

Hugh Hudson

I was shooting a scene in *Chariots of Fire* with John and Lindsay Anderson, who were old friends. Before the first take Lindsay was very nervous. He went over to John, who was sitting very relaxed with *The Times*, probably doing the crossword, and said: 'John, can we read our lines together?' John slowly looked up and said: 'No, I know my lines, thank you.'

Michael Winner

One day while we were filming *The Wicked Lady* he was standing among an enormous crowd of people. Suddenly he said: 'I could be at home watching *Starsky and Hutch*.'

Mavis Walker

After he had completed those scenes in the gas chamber for *War and Remembrance*, I told him how terribly moving I had found them. 'Yes,' he said, 'and what's more I even managed to finish the crossword.'

Martyn Friend

During the filming of *Summer's Lease* for television, one scene involved him making an amusing entrance with the sound of a toilet flushing behind. When I described it to him he immediately retorted: 'Ah, you want the old queen coming out of the closet, do you?'

ॐ

He once turned down a chance to direct a film.

Michael Denison
Over a meal in the Ivy I asked him
if he might be willing to direct *The
Importance of Being Earnest*. 'Oh no, I
don't think so,' he said. 'I seem to have
been doing *The Importance* all my life.
In any case I don't think it would make
a film.' There was a pause, and then he
said: 'It might be rather fun to do it in
Chinese.'

❧

*He was an inveterate filmgoer himself, with a catholic
taste, a sharp critical eye, and a penchant for the mildly
pornographic films to be found around Soho.*

*To Peggy Ashcroft, after walking out of the Hollywood
film of* Romeo and Juliet:
For unspeakable vulgarity, appalling hammery and utter
silliness, I have seen nothing worse, except the ten minutes of
the film of the *Dream*, which I also failed to survive for long.
I should not dream of jeering at the acting of Leslie Howard
and Norma Shearer, for I didn't wait for them to begin, but
Edna May Oliver and John Barrymore, who is like a monstrous
old male impersonator jumping through a hoop, should really
have been shot. *(L)*

Tony Palmer
After watching the full-length version of my *Wagner* film
that he played in, he was fulsome in his praise of his protégé
Richard Burton. Then he added: 'Pity you can hear
him breathe.'

To Jonathan Cecil, during rehearsals for
Halfway Up the Tree*:*
Have you seen the film *Lust in the Swamps*?
It's not very good.

To Roy Dotrice, after going to see Splendour in the
Grass *during rehearsals for* The Cherry Orchard*:*
I can't remember the name of the film – it was something like
Splendid Up the Arse.

8

A Very Naughty Boy

At 75:

'At my age it's all's quiet on the Y-front.'

*Sex and allied matters were among
his favourite subjects for humour.*

Donald Sinden

When he was touring *Hamlet* in India, I met him in Bombay. I asked him what he thought were the essential qualities of acting. He replied: 'I would say feeling and timing.' Then with a wicked smile he added: 'I understand it's the same in many other walks of life.'

Frank Hodge

We were in the library of Farnborough Hall in Oxfordshire, filming the TV series *Six Centuries of Verse*. During a lull I noticed him relaxing with the latest bodice-ripper by Judith Krantz. I asked him what the book was like, to which he replied: 'Oh you would love it – a fuck every four pages!'

Derek Jacobi

We were filming the lists scene in *Richard II* for television. I had this curled hair-do. As the camera started to pan, he said: 'Wonderful blow-job they've done on your hair, dear.' That ruined the take, and they had to start again.

To Bill Hays, who during the shooting of Time After Time *mentioned the 'hair in the gate' in the camera:*
Is it pubic?

To John Mortimer, on a critical review by Kenneth Tynan:
Tynan said I only had two gestures, the left hand up, the right hand up. What did he want me to do, bring out my prick? *(M)*

*To Alec Guinness, on Michael Redgrave's
alleged predilection for bondage:*
Arthur Macrae made me laugh last night by
saying Michael Redgrave's theme song ought to be:
'Some day I'll find you / Both hands behind you!' *(L)*

To Cecil Beaton, after a visit to the Mysore Palace in India:
The elephants all got violent erections, and we had to shroud
our ladies in cloaks and admire the surrounding scenery to
conceal our fascinated amazement. *(L)*

*To his mother, while putting on a wartime ENSA
show for the troops in Gibraltar:*
Bea Lillie went to kick off a football match
on Saturday, and was greeted with a mighty
shout of 'Up ENSA', which would have
pleased Basil Dean, though we thought there
was a tinge of malice behind it! *(L)*

David Hemmings
While we were filming *The Charge of the Light Brigade*
in Turkey, an inaccurate rumour had spread that Tony
Richardson was having an affair with Jill Bennett. One
day a large Russian dancing bear broke loose from its
tether, and started to lumber after the terrified actress.
Gielgud looked up and cried out: 'Oh! Mr Richardson,
how *could* you! And in your motoring-coat too!' *(I)*

Hugh Hudson
While we were preparing to film the dinner scene in *Chariots
of Fire* with Ben Cross, I put some rather large sticks of
asparagus on their plates. John got very excited. 'You're very
naughty Hugh, giving me asparagus – and such big ones!'

Richard Mervyn
While we were filming *The English Garden* I asked him if he
had ever done a commercial. He said he had a wonderful
by-line for an underpants advertisement: 'At my age it's all's
quiet on the Y-front.'

To John Gorrie, after efforts to televise
The Tempest *for the BBC fell through:*
We must find something else to do together
another time, as the girl said to the soldier. *(L)*

Robert Lindsay

While we were on the set at Pinewood shooting *Loser Takes All* there was a delay, so he persuaded his dresser to get him a half bottle of champagne. While we drank it he said: 'They've just done the toilets up in pale blue at the Garrick. It looks very beautiful. The only trouble is, it makes your cock look very shabby.' We got the giggles so badly it stopped the filming.

Bill Hays

During the filming of *Quatermaine's Terms* he was standing in front of a fireplace. Looking through the camera I saw there was a vase on the mantelpiece. I asked if it could be moved six inches. 'Ah, those vitally important six inches!' he said.

Richard Eyre

The director asked him to improvise during a rehearsal of *Volpone*. He was standing at the side of the stage with Ian Charleson. Stuck for something to say, he said, very audibly: 'Yon gentleman has a frightfully large cock.'

To Peter Hall, during rehearsals for Pinter's No Man's Land*:* I never pause in the West End. The first time I played there I took a big pause, and a woman cried out in the balcony, 'Oh! You beast! You've come all over my umbrella!' *(Tim Pigott-Smith)*

ॐ

Nudity was an aspect of life
that invariably tickled his fancy.

To Roy Plomley:
It was rather amusing on the *Caligula* set in Italy to be there
with all the nude extras who, the moment the bell went for
lunch, rushed to have pizzas with their families, clutching
their hands in front of their private parts. *(I)*

Robin Hawdon
We were dining with him in the magnificent Liverpool Adelphi
Hotel, and he was telling highly entertaining theatre stories,
when he broke off and said: 'Oh, look at those two ladies
behind the cash desk.' We looked, and there were two heads
showing just above the high panelled desk at the side of the
restaurant. 'They look as if they're in a Turkish bath,' he went
on, and then giggling said: 'Wouldn't it be wonderful if they
came out from behind there and they were stark naked!'

To Pat and Michael York, on filming Prospero's Books:
I was at first a bit surprised by the hundreds of stark
naked attendants, male and female of all ages and sizes,
but one got quite used to ignoring – and not staring at!
– all the surprising varieties on view. *(L)*

To Christopher Fry, on appearing naked himself in the same film:
It's a most satisfactory feeling, like beating the taxman. *(L)*

To Alec Guinness, passing on a story from the
critic Alexander Woollcott, about Alfred Lunt and Lynn Fontanne
working out their dream production of Macbeth:
Lady M was to pass along the gallery to murder Duncan
stark naked! 'How?' I asked. 'Oh,' said Woollcott, 'behind a
high balustrade, so that her pudenda were still kept strictly
for Alfred's edification!' *(L)*

Bill Hays
He was filming a scene in *War and Remembrance*,
in which he had to be thrown on to the concrete
floor at Auschwitz, with several naked men falling
on top of him. The director Dan Curtis asked him
if he minded doing it again. 'Oh bliss!' he said.

To Noël Coward, who had sent him flowers
for his dressing-room in Brighton:
Your azalea was a dream of beauty, but as soon
as it saw me undressed – and I really cannot blame
it – it withered and shrank, like a parable in the Bible! *(L)*

Helen Osborne
We were both guests of Tony Richardson in the south of
France, and lunching at a beach in St Tropez. Topless was
the new rage. I felt embarrassed, under-endowed, and very
English. 'Go on risk it,' he said. 'If you do it, I'll take off my
sun hat.'

To Emlyn Williams:

I've got rather a good idea for the *Dream*: to do it nude, or as near as one could go. Wouldn't it be superb! With everybody starkers we could just call it *Bottom*. *(M)*

Gielgoodies: A Mixed Bag

Some gaffes have come down to posterity in different versions, most notably those involving the actress Athene Seyler and the actor Clive Morton. Several versions of his famous Eddie Knoblock gaffe are in circulation, but he himself seems to have been guilty of embellishing the story.

Talking at a dinner party about the performance of an elderly actress:
She was as dreadful as poor dear Athene on a very bad night. Oh, not *you*, Athene dear. Another Athene. *(S)*

Michael Kilgarriff
He was recording a radio play in a BBC studio with several distinguished older actors. During a technical break he began fulminating about the inadequate voice-training of young actors. 'The trouble is the youngsters nowadays cannot speak, and we're all getting too old, we're getting past it – all the Sybils and Ediths and Athenes and – Oh, not *you* Athene, dear...'

Margaret Harris
There was one terrible occasion in his dressing-room, when he was talking about an actor, and said: 'He's a terrible bore, almost as much of a bore as dear old Edith – Oh, I'm sorry, Edith!'

After glancing at Clive Morton as he came into
his dressing-room during a provincial tour:
Thank *goodness* it's you! For one dreadful moment I thought
it was going to be that ghastly old bore Clive Morton. *(S)*

Trevor Baxter

Clive Morton told me that while lunching in the canteen at
the BBC Television Centre, Gielgud, carrying his own lunch
on a tray, had passed him, then stopped, stared, went on a
few paces, retraced his steps, stared again, and then said:
'I'm terribly sorry. I thought you were that terrible old bore
Clive Morton.'

Bill Hays

We were with a group of people who wanted to hear
the Eddie Knoblock story. 'You tell it, Bill,' he said.
'You're better at it than me.' So I did. But I forgot the
middle bit, so I made it up. 'I don't remember that bit,'
he said afterwards. 'Can I use it?'

❦

There were many variations on this
brick-dropping theme.

David Storey

Ralph Richardson told me that at a party after a performance of *Home* in New York he said to a woman sitting next to him on a sofa: 'I hear the person to avoid here is a Mrs Higinbotham.' She said: 'But *I* am Mrs Higinbotham.' And he replied: 'I mean the *other* Mrs Higinbotham.'

Peter Shaffer

In Washington during the run of *Five-Finger Exercise*, he took me by the arm and walked me across the vestibule of the hotel, saying: 'You really mustn't listen to Peter Shaffer in rehearsals: he sits up far too late and drinks too much coffee.' And I said: 'I actually went to bed about half-past nine last night, and I don't like coffee.' And he said: 'I wasn't talking about you,' and disappeared into the lift.

Geoffrey Toone

He was in a taxi in New York with Margolot Gilmore, and told her he couldn't bear a certain actor, 'because he's a great friend of Margolot's – oh! not you, Margolot!' – as if there were another one.

Derek Granger
Richard Burton told Laurence Olivier that when he and
Elizabeth Taylor dined with John, he told them he had
recently had lunch with Michael Wilding, one of Elizabeth's
ex-husbands. 'Such a charming man,' he said. 'I can't
imagine how he got mixed up with all those dreadful tarts.'
Elizabeth said: 'John, I was one of them.'

Donald Sinden
In the wings during a performance of *Forty Years On*, Nora
Nicholson asked him where she might take a friend to dinner
that evening. 'There's a local Chinese restaurant that's very
good for second-class people,' he replied, quite forgetting he
had taken her there the night before.

Peter Sallis
We met outside the Strand Theatre, which had huge
blown-up pictures of me and Honor Blackman appearing
there in *Wait Until Dark*. And he said: 'What are you doing at
the moment?' So I looked at him, and then I looked up at all
these posters and bills, and said: 'Well, I'm in *this*.' 'Ah,' he
said, 'I hear the girl's very good.' *(M)*

☙

Sometimes he failed to keep in check
his feelings about his great rival Laurence Olivier.

Siân Phillips
Judi Dench and I went to see him backstage after a
performance of *No Man's Land*, and told him he was
wonderful. 'Oh, do you think so?' he said.
'I'm so lucky to be doing it. It's only because poor
Larry is dead – I mean dying – I mean so much
better, thank God.'

ɞ

He was usually hot on names, but there were exceptions.
Occasionally he pulled back from the brink just in time,
or caused only minimal damage.

To Jane Howell, bumping into her at the BBC:
Ah! Glenda, wonderful speech in the House last night.

To Pat and Michael York:
Did I tell you of the awful moment when Princess Grace
came round in New York, and for one ghastly second I
almost greeted her as Deborah Kerr. I wonder if she guessed,
as she tactfully mentioned Monaco a few seconds later,
which caused the penny to drop with a fearsome clunk. *(L)*

At a read-through of *Julius Caesar* I mistook Brian Cox for an instant for Albert Finney. I said: 'Where are you living now?' and he said: 'Fulham.' I felt sure I had made a mistake. Mind you, they're not altogether unlike. *(I)*

❧

Some gaffes were potentially more wounding than others.

Patrick Garland

He once asked a young actor where he was spending Christmas. 'I'm going to have a wonderful Christmas,' the enthusiastic youngster replied, 'I'm spending it with the Oliviers.' 'With the *Oliviers*!' John replied. 'But they don't even *like* you!'

Siân Phillips

Peter O'Toole was being driven through Portland Place when he saw John walking along, looking lost and not his usual spruce self. He got the chauffeur to stop the car and asked if he could take him anywhere. 'No, no,' said John, who explained that he'd come from the funeral of Binkie Beaumont, the head of HM Tennent. O'Toole said: 'John, you're upset; please let me take you somewhere – anywhere. Have the car.' 'No, no, I'll be all right.' 'Well, if you're sure...' 'Oh, yes – thank you.' As they were about to pull away John tapped on the window, then said: 'You know dear boy, you're not nearly as awful as people make you out to be.'

Opening an exhibition of their work in
the presence of the three Motley designers:
And then there's Elizabeth Montgomery, the prettiest
of the Motleys.... *(David Gothard)*

To radio producer Hallam Tennyson,
who complained he never visited him any more:
No, I used to enjoy coming to your house when your father
was alive.

Martin Jarvis
At the reception after the first night of the stage recital
of Milton's *Paradise Lost* I heard him introducing Gordon
Honeycombe (at that time the nation's favourite newsreader)
to a local dignitary. 'This is the awful man who reads the news
on television – no, no, I mean the man who reads the awful
news on television.' *(M)*

George Baker
When I was running the Theatre Royal in Bury St Edmunds
I asked him if he might come and play Sir Peter Teazle in *The
School for Scandal*. 'No, but do ask me again,' he replied. 'I've
done sillier things in my time.'

To Siân Phillips, cast as Frieda Lawrence in a television series:
I hear you're about to play that ghastly German cow. She's
so boring, and you're quite wrong for it.

Journalists also came in for their share of dropped bricks.

To Mark Amory, at the end of an interview:
I do find these interviews a bore, don't you? *(I)*

To Michael Coveney,
one of the contributors to a celebratory
book of essays published for his eightieth birthday:
It's a frightful book, embarrassing
from beginning to end. *(I)*

To Robert Tanitch, who had presented him with a copy
of an illustrated book he had compiled on his career:
Such witty captions. Did you write them all yourself?

John Heilpern
I bumped into him soon after I had interviewed him and Ralph
Richardson while they were playing in *No Man's Land*. He
gave me an affectionate kiss and said: 'Didn't we all have fun
together during that perfectly *dreadful* interview – I mean
fascinating interview!'

ↇ

Occasionally whole countries were the butt
of his careless remarks.

To John Heilpern:
Someone like Sybil Thorndike never forgets anybody. She even remembers people she met in Australia. *(I)*

Michael Kilgarriff
The Thatcher government had decided to cancel the Theatre Museum project. In the middle of the many protests taking place I heard him say on the radio: 'It's a dreadful thing to do. After all, British theatre is universally renowned and admired and respected. It's one of the great glories of our national life. Every civilised country in the world has a theatre museum – even Holland.'

During a television programme in which he appeared in the American Mid West, when he was asked to name someone who had got him started in the theatre:
It was a wonderful man called Claude Rains, who showed me a great deal when I was at the Royal Academy of Dramatic Art. I think he failed, and went to America. *(Peter Ustinov)*

❧

*When it came to questions of race
and gender, he was the supreme innocent.*

*To Noël Coward, reporting on the
rehearsals of* Nude with Violin
*in front of the company, which
included the black actor Thomas Baptiste:*
We've been working like blacks –
not your kind of black of course, Tommy. *(U)*

*To a mixed-race audience in Southern
Rhodesia, after a performance of* Richard II:
I want to thank all the people in this theatre, back and front,
who have worked like blacks – I mean, who have worked
extremely hard. *(Geoffrey Bayldon)*

*To Merula Salaman, waiting in the wings while
playing Shylock in* The Merchant of Venice:
I don't know how to play a Jew. You're one: how do
you do it? *(Alec Guinness)*

Margaret Harris
He said to me before one production: 'I thought I'd ask
Roger Furse to do the sets, because after all you're only
women at Motley.'

Ion Trewin
When I told him that Hilary Spurling had asked
if she might write his biography, he said: 'Not a *woman*!'

Judy Gielgud
When I finally got a first-class degree after his brother
Val my husband died, he said: 'Now you'll be able to
get a nice job as someone's secretary.'

Thelma Holt
I read a Yeats poem at a memorial service for Toby
Rowland, which I also organised. He wrote me an absolutely
wonderful letter, saying how well the memorial went. At the
bottom of the first page he was saying how well I had read
the poem. However, when I turned over to the next page it
began 'for a woman.'

ɛ৲ɔ

*Many of his bricks were dropped
in the privacy of his dressing-room.*

David Storey
A group came round from the Nigerian National Theatre, four
tall, dignified male figures in traditional costume. John was at
the mirror taking off his make-up, and said to them: 'What's
your next production?' 'It's *Othello*,' one of them replied.
'And will you be blacking up?' he asked. Then he looked up,
saw them in the mirror for the first time, and in horror said:
'Oh, I can see that won't be necessary.'

To the actress Phyllis Calvert,
calling out across a crowded dressing-room:
Goodbye, Phyllis. So glad the hysterectomy went well.
(Angus Mackay)

Hugh Whitemore
I took my young son Tom round after a matinee of
The Best of Friends. 'Did you eat before the show?' John
asked Tom. 'Yes,' he replied, 'we went to the Dumpling
Inn.' And John said: 'Oh the Dumpling Inn. You
should avoid that. They have rats there.'

To a politician from Uganda,
who had been exiled from his native country:
How nice to see you. Are you staying long in England?
(Dirk Bogarde)

❧

Social occasions and birthdays provided further
opportunities for causing offence.

Monica Grey
At one party he went round introducing me to everybody,
saying: 'Have you met Monica, Val's latest wife?'

To his first biographer Ronald Hayman,
after his wife had cooked them a meal:
Delicious. Now I see why you married her.

To the company appearing in the television
version of Antigone, *on realising the director*
Don Taylor had organised a birthday party for him:
Another bloody cake and another bloody present!
(Juliet Stevenson)

ↁ

He himself was occasionally the victim of a gaffe,
one of them self-inflicted.

Talking to Kathleen Tynan, who asked
him during the run of his production of Private Lives:
Have you seen that ghastly performance Maggie Smith
is giving? *(U)*

To Hugh Wheeler:
I met Gloria Swanson at a party – she seems quite a little old
monster, and killed me by saying (not knowing I had done
the production): 'Dear Blanche Thebom begged me to go to
Covent Garden on Friday to see *The Trojans*, but she told me
not to dream of arriving before 7.45, as the first one and a
half hours would bore me stiff!' *(L)*

To Daniel Massey, during the run of The Gay Lord Quex:
I hear your show is coming off. No good? Oh my God,
I directed it! *(Judi Dench)*

9

A World of His Own

'One ought to keep in touch with ordinary
people – if only by an occasional bus ride.'

*His obsession with the theatre left him largely unaware
of the goings-on in the real world, especially anything
remotely connected with politics or current events.*

Richard Attenborough
I was there when he attended a formal lunch at the Mansion House. He was almost tongue-tied. Clement Atlee, then prime minister, was by his side. They were both as monosyllabic as each other. After a while he turned to Atlee and said: 'Where are you living now?'

To Margaret Thatcher, after sitting next to her at a lunch:
I do so hope Mr Heath will prove helpful to you in your campaign. *(L)*

To John Miller, after attending a formal lunch at the Guildhall, where he had been seated between Harold Wilson and James Callaghan, and opposite Jo Grimond:
I didn't know what to talk about: I can't tell the Tories from the Whigs. *(I)*

To John Cornwell:
I went to lunch at Chequers, and Mr Major was so polite and sweet. *(I)*

Peter Shaffer
When war was declared in September
1939 he was alleged to have said to
John Perry: 'It's going to have a
terrible effect on the box-office.'

*To Alec Guinness, looking up at the unmanned
barrage balloons during the Blitz on London:*
Oh dear, our poor boys must be
terribly *lonely* up there. *(M)*

☙

*Certain moments and observations underlined his
somewhat sheltered and privileged life.*

David Storey
He and Ralph Richardson were rehearsing my play *Home*
at the Royal Court, when two cleaning ladies came in to the
gallery, talking loudly. John stopped, looked up in horror,
and called out: 'Cleaning ladies! Cleaning ladies!' He then
turned to Ralph and said: 'How does one talk to these
people?

John Mortimer

When my daughter Emily was a baby we went to dinner with Tony Richardson. We put her in the spare room in her carry cot. After dinner we were taking her out when John said: 'Why didn't you leave that baby at home? Were you afraid of burglars?'

To Oliver Cotton:

Do you have someone who comes in and does for you? I do so loathe making my own bed.

To Richard Findlater:

I don't think the chauffeur-driven life is a very good thing for actors. One ought to keep in touch with ordinary people – if only by an occasional bus ride. *(I)*

To Roy Plomley

I enjoy very much playing butlers, valets and clergymen, but I can't get the accent of a manual worker – perhaps because I've never been one, and I don't suppose I ever shall be now. *(I)*

❦

There were times when his notorious lack
of practical skills came in handy.

Peter Shaffer
After having lunch with John and his partner Martin Hensler
in his rented apartment in New York, I felt tired, so he
suggested I have a nap. As I passed through the hallway I
noticed a fish tank full of turtles, palpably dead. Just as I was
closing my eyes I heard a squeal of fury from Martin: 'Oh
look at my turtles! They've been massacred!' And John said:
'Don't look at me, I've done nothing. I don't even know how
they work.'

❧

Sometimes his head was well and truly in the clouds.

Nigel Hawthorne
One night he was in his dressing-room after a performance
when there was a knock at the door. 'Yes,' he said, 'who is
it?' 'John dear, it's Yehudi.' 'Yehudi who?'

Timothy Bateson
He was once asked at Stratford why he had told a journalist
about the forthcoming season before the artistic director
Anthony Quayle could make the official announcement. 'The
man kindly asked me,' he said, 'so I told him.'

Peter Shaffer

John was in the sea at the Lido in Venice. His way of swimming was to stand with the water only up to his ankles, but to do the breast stroke with his arms. He would walk up and down in the shallows like an African wading bird. My mother went up to him and said: 'Good morning, Sir John. I'm Peter Shaffer's mother.' And John said: 'You could well be right!' and went on walking.

&

His innate shyness could prompt him to make unexpected remarks.

Julian Glover

He was standing in a full lift at Broadcasting House, obviously very nervous and self-conscious. Suddenly he announced: 'My brother's head of drama here.'

Peter Ustinov

Peter Jones went up to the Tennent office to see John. He was lying on the sofa like Madame Recamier, and said to Peter: 'We've never met, but I've seen you in the street.'

Isla Blair:

When I was introduced to him he said: 'You are very delighted to meet me.'

John Theocharis
Coming out of Broadcasting House we came across professional autograph-hunters of a certain age. He signed their books and then, evidently feeling that he had to say something else, he said: 'What else do you do?'

Judi Dench
He was doing a Priestley play in the BBC rehearsal rooms, and invited several of us to join him for lunch in the canteen, all devotees. We sat down and waited for him to say something. There was a pause, and then he said: 'Have any of you had any obscene phone calls?'

10

Senior Moments

On his ninetieth birthday:
> 'Most of my friends seem either to be
> dead, extremely deaf, or living in the
> wrong part of Kent.'

*Even in old age – he lived until he was 96 – he
retained his merry sense of humour.*

To Richard Findlater:
Most of the scripts I get sent nowadays are about a man at death's door. I suppose it's a useful rehearsal for the real thing. *(I)*

To journalists and friends assembled in the foyer of the Lyric theatre, which was being re-named the Gielgud:
For the last two or three years I have walked up and down Shaftesbury Avenue and haven't been able to recognise any of the names on the bills outside the theatre. Now I will know at least one name. *(I)*

To Noël Coward:
Far too many people ill or dying lately. The spring seems to finish them off. We are all getting painfully senior. Shall we lunch or sup while you are here – while we are both still here? *(L)*

To Ralph Richardson:
David Hockney did a drawing of me when I was 70, and I thought if I really look like that I must kill myself tomorrow. *(John Heilpern)*

To Hugh Wheeler, after dining with David Webster:
David's teeth appeared to be rather here and there – they are beginning to droop a little, I fear, despite all their riches. Aren't we all? *(L)*

To Brian Case:
It's so boring saying one mustn't smoke, one mustn't eat eggs, one must wear a seat belt. There is almost nothing left except sex, and I'm too old for that unfortunately. *(I)*

❧

Even death was a subject he was able to treat with a light touch.

To John Cornwell, on the risk of accepting film roles in his old age:
If I die on the job they'll give it to Michael Denison, and I couldn't bear that. *(I)*

To Gyles Brandreth, on his contemporaries:
Most of my friends seem either to be dead, extremely deaf, or living in the wrong part of Kent. *(B)*

On reciting poetry at countless memorial services:
So many of my erstwhile friends have plaques at St Paul's in Covent Garden, I feel it is hardly worth my while to go home. *(S)*

To Mike Hutchinson:
Death? Sometimes I think people see it as an indecent race between me, the Pope and Boris Yeltsin. *(I)*

To David Lewin:
I'd rather like to die in England. The graveyards are much friendlier here than in America. *(I)*

On his last wishes:
I've left strict instructions for no memorial service. They have become society functions. *(S)*

ભ

In his final years he was thoroughly aware of his notorious tactlessness.

To George Pitcher, on the occasion of his eightieth birthday:
The Garrick Club is giving me a great dinner in April. And of course I shall have to make a speech and try not to weep or drop any notable bricks. *(L)*

ભ

But he still continued to drop them.

To his agent Paul Lyon-Maris,
who asked him what it felt like to be ninety:
The terrible thing is that people keep asking you what it feels like to be ninety.

To Gyles Brandreth, who had asked him to lunch at the House of Commons to celebrate his ninetieth birthday:
I'm delighted to have been asked. You see, all my *real* friends are dead. *(B)*

Index